P9-EMR-693

TINA
TURNER

TINA TURNER

❧

Judy L. Hasday, Ed.M.

HARBORFIELDS PUBLIC LIBRARY

CHELSEA HOUSE PUBLISHERS
Philadelphia

3 0632 00057 3463

For my grandmother, G. Jean Fairbanks, in loving memory:

Grandparents are a very special link in the family, from childhood through adulthood, and you were there to share in every milestone with me. Thank you for all the years of caring support, laughs, and inspiration you gave so lovingly.

I miss you every day, as I do Pops, but I carry you both in my thoughts and my heart always.

Chelsea House Publishers

Editor in Chief	Stephen Reginald
Production Manager	Pamela Loos
Director of Photography	Judy L. Hasday
Art Director	Sara Davis
Managing Editor	James D. Gallagher
Senior Production Editor	LeeAnne Gelletly

Staff for TINA TURNER

Project Editor	Therese De Angelis
Contibuting Editor	James D. Gallagher
Associate Art Director	Takeshi Takahashi
Designer	21st Century Publishing and Communications
Picture Researcher	Patricia Burns
Cover Illustrator	Bradford Brown

© 2000 by Chelsea House Publishers, a division of Main Line Book Co. All rights reserved. Printed and bound in the United States of America.

The Chelsea House World Wide Website address is
http://www.chelseahouse.com

First Printing

1 3 5 7 9 8 6 4 2

Library of Congress Cataloging-in-Publication Data

Hasday, Judy L., 1957–
Tina Turner / Judy L. Hasday.
104 pp. cm.—(Black Americans of Achievement)
Discography: p. 99.
Includes bibliographical references (p. 100) and index.
Summary: Traces the life and career of Tina Turner, from the early days of the Ike and Tina Turner Revue, through the years of spousal abuse, to the success of Grammy Awards and film work.
ISBN 0-7910-4967-1 (hc) — ISBN 0-7910-4968-X (pb)
1. Turner, Tina—Juvenile literature. 2. Rock musicians—United States—Biography—Juvenile literature. [1. Turner, Tina. 2. Singers. 3. Afro-Americans—Biography. 4. Women—Biography. 5. Rock music.] I. Title. II. Series.
ML3930.T87H37 1999
782.42166'092—dc21
[B]
                                                              99-13359
                                                                  CIP
                                                                   AC

Frontis: Tina Turner's powerful voice and incredible onstage energy combine to make her the Queen of Rock and Roll.

CONTENTS

BLACK AMERICANS OF ACHIEVEMENT

HENRY AARON
baseball great

KAREEM ABDUL-JABBAR
basketball great

MUHAMMAD ALI
heavyweight champion

RICHARD ALLEN
*religious leader and
social activist*

MAYA ANGELOU
author

LOUIS ARMSTRONG
musician

ARTHUR ASHE
tennis great

JOSEPHINE BAKER
entertainer

JAMES BALDWIN
author

TYRA BANKS
model

BENJAMIN BANNEKER
scientist and mathematician

AMIRI BARAKA
poet and playwright

COUNT BASIE
bandleader and composer

ROMARE BEARDEN
artist

JAMES BECKWOURTH
frontiersman

MARY MCLEOD BETHUNE
educator

GEORGE WASHINGTON
CARVER
botanist

CHARLES CHESNUTT
author

JOHNNIE COCHRAN
lawyer

BILL COSBY
entertainer

PAUL CUFFE
merchant and abolitionist

MILES DAVIS
musician

FATHER DIVINE
religious leader

FREDERICK DOUGLASS
abolitionist editor

CHARLES DREW
physician

W. E. B. DU BOIS
scholar and activist

PAUL LAURENCE DUNBAR
poet

DUKE ELLINGTON
bandleader and composer

RALPH ELLISON
author

JULIUS ERVING
basketball great

LOUIS FARRAKHAN
political activist

ELLA FITZGERALD
singer

MORGAN FREEMAN
actor

MARCUS GARVEY
black nationalist leader

JOSH GIBSON
baseball great

WHOOPI GOLDBERG
entertainer

CUBA GOODING JR.
actor

ALEX HALEY
author

PRINCE HALL
social reformer

JIMI HENDRIX
musician

MATTHEW HENSON
explorer

GREGORY HINES
performer

BILLIE HOLIDAY
singer

LENA HORNE
entertainer

WHITNEY HOUSTON
singer and actress

LANGSTON HUGHES
poet

ZORA NEALE HURSTON
author

JANET JACKSON
singer

JESSE JACKSON
civil-rights leader and politician

MICHAEL JACKSON
entertainer

SAMUEL L. JACKSON
actor

T. D. JAKES
religious leader

JACK JOHNSON
heavyweight champion

MAGIC JOHNSON
basketball great

SCOTT JOPLIN
composer

BARBARA JORDAN
politician

MICHAEL JORDAN
basketball great

CORETTA SCOTT KING
civil-rights leader

MARTIN LUTHER KING JR.
civil-rights leader

LEWIS LATIMER
scientist

SPIKE LEE
filmmaker

CARL LEWIS
champion athlete

JOE LOUIS
heavyweight champion

RONALD MCNAIR
astronaut

MALCOLM X
militant black leader

BOB MARLEY
musician

THURGOOD MARSHALL
Supreme Court justice

TONI MORRISON
author

ELIJAH MUHAMMAD
religious leader

EDDIE MURPHY
entertainer

JESSE OWENS
champion athlete

SATCHEL PAIGE
baseball great

CHARLIE PARKER
musician

ROSA PARKS
civil-rights leader

COLIN POWELL
military leader

PAUL ROBESON
singer and actor

JACKIE ROBINSON
baseball great

CHRIS ROCK
comedian/actor

DIANA ROSS
entertainer

WILL SMITH
actor

CLARENCE THOMAS
Supreme Court justice

SOJOURNER TRUTH
antislavery activist

HARRIET TUBMAN
antislavery activist

NAT TURNER
slave revolt leader

TINA TURNER
entertainer

DENMARK VESEY
slave revolt leader

ALICE WALKER
author

MADAM C. J. WALKER
entrepreneur

BOOKER T. WASHINGTON
educator

DENZEL WASHINGTON
actor

J. C. WATTS
politician

VANESSA WILLIAMS
singer and actress

OPRAH WINFREY
entertainer

TIGER WOODS
golf star

RICHARD WRIGHT
author

ON
ACHIEVEMENT

———— ❧ ————

Coretta Scott King

Before you begin this book, I hope you will ask yourself what the word *excellence* means to you. I think it's a question we should all ask, and keep asking as we grow older and change. Because the truest answer to it should never change. When you think of excellence, perhaps you think of success at work; or of becoming wealthy; or meeting the right person, getting married, and having a good family life.

Those goals are worth striving for, but there is a better way to look at excellence. As Martin Luther King Jr. said in one of his last sermons, "I want you to be first in love. I want you to be first in moral excellence. I want you to be first in generosity. If you want to be important, wonderful. If you want to be great, wonderful. But recognize that he who is greatest among you shall be your servant."

My husband knew that the true meaning of achievement is service. When I met him, in 1952, he was already ordained as a Baptist minister and was working toward a doctoral degree at Boston University. I was studying at the New England Conservatory and dreamed of accomplishments in music. We married a year later, and after I graduated the following year we moved to Montgomery, Alabama. We didn't know it then, but our notions of achievement were about to undergo a dramatic change.

You may have read or heard about what happened next. What began with the boycott of a local bus line grew into a national crusade, and by the time he was assassinated in 1968 my husband had fashioned a black movement powerful enough to shatter forever the practice of racial segregation. What you may not have read about is where he learned to resist injustice without compromising his religious beliefs.

He adopted a strategy of nonviolence from a man of a different race, who lived in a different country and even practiced a different religion. The man was Mahatma Gandhi, the great leader of India, who devoted his life to serving humanity in the spirit of love and nonviolence. It was in these principles that Martin discovered his method for social reform. More than anything else, those two principles were the key to his achievements.

These books are about African Americans who served society through the excellence of their achievements. They form part of the rich history of black men and women in America—a history of stunning accomplishments in every field of human endeavor, from literature and art to science, industry, education, diplomacy, athletics, jurisprudence, even polar exploration.

Not all of the people in this history had the same ideals, but I think you will find that all of them had something in common. Like Martin Luther King Jr., they all decided to become "drum majors" and serve humanity. In that principle—whether it was expressed in books, inventions, or song—they found a goal and a guide outside themselves that showed them a way to serve others instead of living only for themselves.

Reading the stories of these courageous men and women not only helps us discover the principles that we will use to guide our own lives; it also teaches us about our black heritage and about America itself. It is crucial for us to know the heroes and heroines of our history and to realize that the price we paid in our struggle for equality in America was dear. But we must also understand that we have gotten as far as we have partly because America's democratic system and ideals made it possible.

We are still struggling with racism and prejudice. But the great men and women in this series are a tribute to the spirit of the country in which they have flourished. And that makes their stories special and worth knowing.

1

AND THE WINNER IS . . .

"[Tina's] just a rocker, man. She's just a rock and roll chick, and she loves rock, and I think that's what drives her."

—Bryan Adams, 1993

Tina Turner gives a high-energy performance of her hit "What's Love Got To Do with It?" during the 1985 Grammy Awards ceremony. Tina was nominated for five Grammys that night, and earned three of the coveted awards.

THE TUESDAY AFTERNOON sun cast a golden glow on the white concrete facade of the Shrine Auditorium in Los Angeles, California. Work had been underway since morning to handle the large crowds and heavy traffic that would make their way to the west Jefferson Boulevard and 32nd Street entrances that afternoon. Through the years, this magnificent Moorish-style structure has hosted many live and televised arts and entertainment events, including the American Ballet, the Academy Awards, and the American Music Awards. On this day, February 26, 1985, the Shrine Auditorium would open its doors for the National Academy of Recording Arts and Sciences' (NARAS) 27th Annual Grammy Awards.

By midafternoon, throngs of fans began to arrive at the Shrine, hoping to catch a glimpse of their favorite celebrities as scores of chauffeured limousines motored down Jefferson Boulevard and dropped off rock, blues, country, and pop music performers and guests attending the awards ceremony. The fans were of all backgrounds and ages: middle-aged housewives, students cutting school, punk rockers with blue hair and pierced navels. All of them pressed against the barricades, hoping to catch a glimpse of a Grammy nominee such as Bruce Springsteen, Lionel Richie, Phil Collins, Prince, newcomer Cyndi Lauper, or Tina Turner—the Queen of Rock and Roll herself.

If NARAS had a Comeback Grammy, it surely would have been awarded to Tina Turner, nearly everyone's sentimental favorite. Tina would have the chance to be the big winner of the evening. The former "high-voltage, shimmy-dancing" half of the Ike and Tina Turner Revue of the 1960s and 1970s, Tina was coming off the best year of her solo career. *Private Dancer*, her first wildly successful solo album, had sailed up the charts immediately after its April 1984 release, reaching number three by September of the same year. Only Bruce Springsteen's blockbuster *Born in the U.S.A.* and Prince's *Purple Rain* ranked higher.

Private Dancer was a success not only in sales, but also with the critics. *Rolling Stone* magazine gave the album a glittering four-star rating. The *Los Angeles Times* said that Tina's gritty voice could "melt vinyl." Ultimately the album would go platinum, selling more than 10 million copies. It remained in the top 100 on the music charts for 71 weeks, yielding five Top 10 singles, including Tina's first-ever number-one single, "What's Love Got To Do with It." Having received five Grammy nominations, including Best Female Rock Vocal Performance, Best Female Pop Vocal Performance, and Record of the Year, the 45-year-old singer looked forward to a night of exciting possibilities.

The 1985 Grammy Awards began with what the *Philadelphia Inquirer* called "a gratifying nod to pop-music history." Huey Lewis and the News kicked off the evening with an a cappella version of the 1963 rhythm-and-blues hit "It's All Right"

Tina Turner, hugged by singer/songwriter Lionel Ritchie, holds the three Grammys she received at the 1985 awards ceremony. Tina was honored for Best Female Rock Vocal Performance (for the song "Better Be Good to Me"), and she won Best Female Pop Vocal Performance and Record of the Year for "What's Love Got To Do with It," her first number-one hit.

by Curtis Mayfield and the Impressions before segueing into its own Grammy-nominated song, "The Heart of Rock and Roll."

Throughout the rest of the evening, audiences were treated to performances by such artists as Kenny Loggins, Stevie Wonder, and the first Grammy winner of the night, Cyndi Lauper. But even the legendary composer and conductor Leonard Bernstein kept his Lifetime Achievement Award acceptance speech brief because, he explained, "it would mean taking one more minute away from guess who? Tina Turner."

Before the evening's telecast, Tina had already won the Grammy for Best Female Rock Vocal Performance for "Better Be Good to Me." Awards ceremony host John Denver announced her stage performance. "So let's see, 'River Deep, Mountain High,' 'Proud

Mary,' 'I Want to Take You Higher' . . . you know who I'm talking about," said Denver. "Here's the explosive, the one and only, Tina Turner!" Clad in an elegant shimmering red mini-gown, the woman described by the *New York Times* as "two sensational legs topped by an explosion of hair" strutted on stage to an enthusiastic outpouring of affection from the audience. After the husky-voiced singer finished performing her hit single "What's Love Got To Do with It," she was rewarded with a thunderous standing ovation. It would truly be a night to remember.

The Grammy Award for Best Female Pop Vocal Performance was announced by co-presenters Andy Summers and Julian Lennon. Nominated along with Tina were Sheila E., Sheena Easton, Cyndi Lauper, and Denice Williams. Before Summers even finished announcing Tina's name, the audience was on its feet, filling the auditorium with cheers and applause.

An elated Tina accepted the award, thanking not only the songwriters and her manager, Roger Davies, but also her fans. "I've been waiting for this opportunity for such a long time," she said. "I want to thank all the people [who] voted for me and all of the viewers [who are] rooting for me, and all of you here this evening. . . . I feel really good. Thank you very much."

Only Chaka Khan's win for Best Female Rhythm-and-Blues Vocal Performance prevented Turner from becoming the first woman to win in three vocal categories in the same year. But there was more to come before the end of this magical night in Tina Turner's life.

The long ceremony came to a close with the announcement of the winner of Record of the Year, the evening's highest honor. Presenting the award was Motown great Diana Ross, who teased the audience before announcing the winner: "What's Love Got To Do with It." The audience was standing before Tina and her producer, Terry Britten, even reached the stage.

Once on stage, Tina, now wearing a slinky black and silver minidress, confessed that she hadn't really liked the title song when she first heard it. "It wasn't my type of song. . . . It wasn't written for me. It's a bit odd, but that's what hit records are about," she said. She looked out at the audience as she continued: "My goodness, this has been a wonderful evening. I'd love to tell everyone just how it really feels, but I don't have the time." While some in the crowd were still yelling, "We love you Tina!" the singer focused her attention on a particular spot in the audience as she continued. "I'd like to take this award and give it to someone that's been wonderful to me as a friend and in business and in many ways, my manager Roger Davies." Tina raised the Grammy award in Roger's direction and said, "It's been a wonderful year."

After the ceremony, Tina Turner shared her reflections on the night's achievements. "You've got to earn one of these," she told the press. "You have to have the material, and now that I've got it I'm starting to get these. . . . You know, I'm really especially happy about this. You have to remember, I never really had a hit record. I've never had a number-one record. So this is really special for me."

Tina's well-earned recognition that night at last blotted out the feelings of loneliness and rejection she had carried from her childhood, as well as the painful memories of the years with her abusive husband, Ike Turner. Tina had come a long way from her childhood home near the strawberry and cotton fields of western Tennessee, and her journey to stardom had only begun.

2

NUT BUSH CITY LIMITS

"Tina was probably a great little performer when she was 3 1/2 years old."

—Mark Knopfler, lead singer
of Dire Straits, 1993

T HE MISSISSIPPI RIVER cuts a natural border between Tennessee and its western neighbor, Arkansas. In Golddust, a small town near the river, you can pick up State Highway 19, which winds its way east-southeast. Soybean, tobacco, strawberry, and cotton fields thrive in the rich Delta soil on either side of the two-lane road. Sandwiched between the towns of Ripley and Brownsville on Highway 19, about 60 miles northwest of Memphis, is the sparsely populated community of Nut Bush. The town's residents, mostly farmers, live relatively unnoticed in the surrounding backwoods and meadows off the road.

In the 1930s Highway 19 meandered through Nut Bush, passing the town's cotton gin, where the yearly crop was cleansed of its seed and processed for baling. Across from the gin was a general store, with the Edders Grove Elementary School a little farther down the road. Next to the school was a small store owned by Miss Alglee Flowler. She sold soda pop and snack foods by day, and in the evenings she provided a place for folks to drink beer and dance to the musical sounds of Mr. Bootsy Whitelow, a trombonist of local fame. And

Travelers on State Highway 19 in Tennessee are welcomed by this sign at the Nut Bush city limits. To the left is the town's cotton gin.

Tina's father, Floyd Richard, was a deacon at the Woodlawn Baptist Church, located near Nut Bush (facing page). Her mother had grown up on the Poindexter farm (above), where Tina's grandparents worked as sharecroppers (tenant farmers who work someone else's land and give the owner a portion of the crops as payment).

of course there was the Woodlawn Baptist Church. Set back from the road a bit, the church served the area's residents with spiritual nourishment every Sunday.

That was pretty much all there was to Nut Bush in 1939. The community's population of whites, blacks, and Native Americans lived in relative harmony, despite the fact that Tennessee, like the rest of the South, was officially segregated. Nut Bush remained an unhurried, tranquil town, largely unaffected by the rumbling sounds of war half a world away.

The woman who would one day be known as Tina Turner was born Anna Mae Bullock on Sunday morning, November 26, 1939, in a small four-room wooden house on a large farm in Nut Bush. Anna Mae was the second child of Floyd Richard (usually called Richard) and Zelma Bullock, who already had a three-year-old daughter, Alline. Richard was the foreman for his white employers, Ruby and Vollye Poindexter, who owned the farm.

Richard was also a deacon at the Woodlawn Baptist Church. He had been raised a God-fearing, Bible-reading Christian whose parents, Roxanna and Alex Bullock, lived a bit farther north on Highway 19, closer to the church. Roxanna was a no-nonsense, stern woman whose life was centered around her church. Richard's father, Alex, however, was an alcoholic who spent many weekends sleeping in his easy chair while his wife and son attended services.

At the other end of Nut Bush lived Zelma's kin, the Curries. Her father, Josephus, was of mixed heritage—one-quarter black and three-quarters Navajo. "Papa Joe," as Josephus was called, worked for many years as a sharecropper on the Poindexter farm. Zelma's mother, Georgianna ("Mama Georgie"), was, like her husband, one-quarter black and three-quarters Native American, but she was of Cherokee blood. Papa Joe and Mama Georgie were warm, loving people who had grown up learning to respect the land they lived and worked on.

Anna Mae's parents, Zelma and Richard, had a turbulent relationship. One of seven children, Zelma was not meek by any means—she learned to shoot pistols and began smoking cigars when she was just 10 years old. As a teen, Zelma gave birth out of wedlock to a baby girl she named Evelyn. Mama Georgie not only raised Evelyn but also cared for Margaret and Joe Melvin Currie, the children of her recently widowed brother, Joe. When Zelma and Richard had an especially bad fight, Zelma too would stay with Papa Joe and Mama Georgie.

Though times were hard, the Bullocks were not as poor as many of their neighbors. Richard grew onions, sweet potatoes, tomatoes, turnips, and cabbage on his acre of land. Chickens and cows provided eggs, fresh milk, and meat. In summer, freshly caught perch added variety to the family's diet, and each fall, three pigs were slaughtered to sustain them through the winter months. Zelma made sure that her family was clean and neatly dressed. Anna Mae and Alline each had their own tidy bedrooms. Anna Mae never felt poor.

One event that the whole town enjoyed was the annual Labor Day picnic. There was plenty of food and drinks for everybody—homemade fried chicken, biscuits, pies, and refreshing ice-cold lemonade that went down easily in the wilting heat. As an extra treat, Mr. Bootsy Whitelow sometimes showed up and played his trombone. At times he was joined by a couple of other musicians. Even as a young child, Anna Mae enjoyed entertaining others. She loved to dance and sing along with the men, and she encouraged others to do the same.

Unfortunately for Anna Mae, gatherings like these were only brief respites from an otherwise lonely childhood. The lively child had been born into a home where no one expressed affection and where there was little love between her parents. She longed to feel close to her mother, who was often cold and out of reach. In her 1986 autobiography, Tina Turner recalled how painful that lack of affection felt, even when she was a toddler: "I loved [my mother] and she didn't even realize it," Tina wrote. "My mother wasn't mean to me, but she wasn't warm, she wasn't close, the way she was with Alline. She just didn't want me. But she was my mother, and I loved her."

The only place where Anna Mae felt genuine love and a sense of belonging was at Mama Georgie and Papa Joe's home, where she could visit her cousins Margaret and Joe Melvin. She knew that her sister loved her, but Alline was not like her; she was quiet and introverted while Anna Mae was energetic and curious, happier climbing trees or investigating the nearby pond than she was trying to sit quietly in lady-like starched dresses. But before long even this small measure of comfort and security would disappear.

On Sunday morning, December 7, 1941, at 7:55 A.M., the Japanese launched an unprovoked surprise attack on the United States, sending more than 350 warplanes to bomb the U.S. Pacific Fleet at Pearl Harbor, Hawaii. The United States immediately declared war on Japan. World War II, until that time a faraway conflict, had now come to America.

As the United States prepared for war, privately owned factories that once manufactured items such as vacuum cleaners or automobile parts were converted to supply materials for ships, planes, and weapons. In addition, the United States was developing a deadly new weapon—the atomic bomb. One of the plants dedicated to producing materials for the bomb was in Oak Ridge, Tennessee, about 360 miles east of Nut Bush. The area was chosen for its abundant water and electric supply, and because the surrounding hills and valleys kept the site mostly hidden from local residents.

For Richard and Zelma, acquiring jobs in Oak Ridge was a chance to escape Nut Bush and earn a good living. Richard got a job with the federal government's bomb project while Zelma took on two jobs, as a waitress and a dormitory maid. But Anna Mae and

The lure of better jobs—and the possibility of a better life—inspired Richard and Zelma Bullock to move to Oak Ridge, Tennessee, in 1942, leaving Anna Mae and Alline with relatives. Richard took a position at the Clinton Engineer Works, where a military project was underway to develop the atomic bomb.

Alline did not accompany their parents. Instead, they were "farmed out" to relatives. Alline would stay with Mama Georgie and Papa Joe. Anna Mae was not as fortunate—she was sent in the other direction, to Roxanna and Alex's house.

Anna Mae was devastated. Not yet four years old, she had been left behind by her parents and separated from her sister. She longed to be with Alline and wanted desperately to live with Mama Georgie and Papa Joe, but she was allowed only occasional visits to see the Currie clan.

Only during these visits did Anna Mae feel like herself. Every time she had to leave the Curries she screamed and cried and tried to run away, but her tantrums never did any good. She was always returned to her father's rigid and strict family. Mama Roxanna believed it was not proper for a young girl to be running around wild. Often she made Anna Mae sit quietly in a chair, doing nothing, or she took her to restrained, sedate church services. Anna Mae felt like a small prisoner.

Finally, in 1944, Alline and Anna Mae were reunited with their parents in Knoxville for one summer. Knoxville was quite a change from Nut Bush—a large, modern city where houses were made of brick and streets were paved. And unlike Nut Bush, a broad variety of stores and shops lined the streets of Knoxville.

Mrs. Blake, a friend of the Bullock's landlady, looked after the girls while their parents worked. Sometimes she took Alline and Anna Mae to her church. There, Anna Mae was introduced to the joyous enthusiasm of the Pentecostal church movement. It was a hand-clapping, foot-stomping, tambourine-thumping style of praise and worship. Sometimes members of the congregation felt so full of the Spirit that they'd start talking in tongues, a strange incoherent kind of babbling that thrilled and baffled Anna Mae. She was electrified by the music she heard—and by the freedom to dance and leap around while worshipping.

The summer in Knoxville passed quickly, however, and the girls were shipped back to Nut Bush. But Anna Mae and Alline didn't feel the same as when they left the town a few months earlier. They had received their first exposure to life beyond Nut Bush, a dynamic, fast-moving world that was far different from the cotton fields of western Tennessee.

3

LEARNING TO SURVIVE

*[Tina] would get up there [on the dressing table stool] and take
her braids down and pull those mirrors together and then look
at herself playin' piano—just pretend, of course, drummin'
her fingers along the top of the table—and singin'. Yes, she had
a beautiful voice, even back then.*

—Zelma Bullock, in *I, Tina*

A family of sharecroppers picks
cotton in a southern field.
After World War II ended,
many African Americans lost
their jobs to white servicemen
returning home from battle.
When Richard's work ended at
Oak Ridge, the Bullock family
returned to Nut Bush and
sharecropping. "I hated it. I
hated picking cotton," his
famous daughter later admitted.

AFTER WORLD WAR II ended, Richard and
Zelma Bullock returned to Nut Bush, retrieved their
daughters, and moved to the nearby town of Flagg
Grove. Richard resumed work as a sharecropper, and
the girls were once again subjected to the constant
squabbling of their parents. In a few years the family
moved again, this time to Spring Hill, another small
town along Highway 19.

By now Anna Mae had started school. Her greatest
sources of comfort and companionship still came from
Alline and Margaret. Though they were both three
years older than Anna Mae, she could talk to them
about almost anything. She and Margaret became
especially close. Unfortunately, they saw one another
only on weekends, when everyone went into Ripley
on Saturday nights for relaxation and entertainment. After dropping off the kids at the Webb
Theater, the adults headed around the corner to the
Hole, the back alley off Washington Street that was

home to several rib joints and other clubs, where they could drink, dance, and unwind. After the movie ended, Anna Mae, Alline, their half-sister Evelyn, Margaret, and Joe Melvin went to the Hole to find the adults.

Often Anna Mae would linger outside the clubs, watching people come and go. She saw the glamorous women dressed in their best clothes and wearing makeup and high heels, and she observed as the grownups danced to boogie-woogie music and made out in cars parked in the nearby lot. At times, the excitement would even erupt into loud shouting matches or fistfights. Anna Mae watched it all—a glimpse into the strange and wonderful world of adulthood.

Though she never felt carefree, Anna Mae had dreams, and they never included picking cotton in the hot southern sun, hauling a bag over her shoulder that weighed as much as she did. In an interview for her documentary video, *Tina Turner: The Girl from Nut Bush*, Tina explained how her aversion to cotton led her to pursue her childhood dreams:

> Oh, I hated it. I hated picking cotton and chopping it. It was, the sun was so hot. . . . I dreaded those times and that's the only thing that made me change my life. I knew that I couldn't do that. That was something that as a child I knew the beginning of dislike and hate and cannot do and don't want to do and will not do. That was my incentive to change my life.

Instead of concentrating on the backbreaking work, Anna Mae preferred to let her mind wander. In her imagination she moved in a world where she didn't have to work so hard or feel so alone, and where her parents didn't fight all the time. She loved pretending, acting out scenes from movies she'd seen at the Webb Theater in Ripley. She loved playing with her hair, often watching herself in the mirror as she styled it. And Anna Mae loved to sing.

The first time she sang formally was with the choir of the Spring Hill Baptist Church. Even as a youngster, she had a strong and beautiful voice. Singing about God or feeling the Spirit did not move her nearly as much as the rhythm of the music she heard. She especially liked the up-tempo songs, the ones that moved people to shouting and swaying.

When Anna Mae was about 11 years old, the fighting between her parents finally came to a head. One day her mother simply left. This time, Zelma did not stay at Mama Georgie's. In fact, she didn't even stay in Tennessee: Richard would later learn that Zelma had moved to St. Louis, Missouri, to live with one of her aunts. Anna Mae knew the day would come when her parents could no longer live together, but she never expected her mother to leave her and Alline behind. Every day she waited for Zelma to return or to send for her daughters. But that never

One of the rib joints in the Hole, a Ripley neighborhood of restaurants, bars, and dance clubs. During visits to the Hole, Anna Mae Bullock caught a glimpse of a world that was much different from life in Nut Bush, and she promised herself that one day she would leave the tiny Tennessee town.

happened. Five years would pass before Anna Mae would see Zelma again.

The pain of being abandoned by her mother never left Anna Mae. "It was dramatic when my mother split," she recalled in *Tina Turner: The Girl from Nut Bush*. "There's something about when a mother leaves. It's fine if the father can sort of drift about, I guess. But when a mother leaves, it leaves some kind of loneliness for a girl." With her mother gone, Anna Mae increasingly looked to her cousin Margaret for guidance. Though only a young girl herself, Margaret became her best friend and teacher, and the mother Zelma couldn't be for her daughter. "She was Godsent, truly," Tina says of her cousin. "You see, I believe that you're always given someone—maybe not a father or a mother or a sister or a brother, but someone. And I was given Margaret. For a while, anyway."

Not long after Zelma's departure, Richard remarried a young divorcée from Ripley named Essie Mae, who brought along her 11-year-old daughter, Nettie Mae, from a previous marriage. Essie Mae and her daughter seemed much more sophisticated than the people Anna Mae was accustomed to being around, and she felt uncomfortable in their presence. She resented the fact that her father treated Essie Mae better than he had ever treated her own mother. The tranquillity didn't last very long, however. The two began fighting regularly, and the marriage ended after about a year.

Lacking the time or inclination to care for his daughters, Richard sought out a caretaker. He left them with a woman named Miss Jonelle while he worked, but when he fought with her, he'd drop Alline and Anna Mae with Mama Roxanna, or with Ella Vera, the mother-in-law of Richard's brother Pick. And then Richard was gone, too. Just as their mother had done, he left without warning, moving to

Detroit and leaving his daughters with Ella Vera.

Anna Mae, now 14, was truly on her own. She got along with Ella Vera but didn't feel particularly close to her. Left to her own devices, she got an after-school job housekeeping and baby-sitting for the Hendersons, a white couple living in Ripley. For the first time in her life, Anna Mae saw what a stable, happy household was like. She enjoyed taking care of David, the Hendersons' baby, and helping Miss Connie around the house. Before long, she was sleeping there over weekends. Watching the way the couple interacted with one another made Anna

Anna Mae always loved to sing. Her first public performances were as a choir member in the Spring Hill Baptist Church.

Lollie Lee Mann (far left), now a member of the Gospel singing group called the Pearlettes, was the first person to sing publicly with Anna Mae Bullock when the two were children.

Mae think for the first time about what marriage and having a family of her own would be like. "I'd never thought about marriage before—not when I was living with my parents, with all their bickering and fighting," Tina Turner recalled in her autobiography. "But the Hendersons' marriage was different. . . . They had their baby and they had their house. And I realized that that was what I wanted too—I wanted that kind of affection and caring and commitment. A real romance."

Although the Hendersons acted as surrogate parents for Anna Mae, she was still happiest when she got to see Margaret, who often came to Ripley with Evelyn on weekends. The teenage Anna Mae turned to Margaret for motherly advice about dating, meeting boys, putting on makeup, and dressing well. Her cousin was the one stable force in Anna

Mae's life. Margaret would always be there—or so Anna Mae thought.

One day in 1954, Margaret told Anna Mae a secret: she was pregnant. She had fallen in love with a boy named Ham Stocking. They had talked about getting married, but that was before she learned she was pregnant. Now Margaret didn't know what to do. Should she have the baby? Should she get married? Should she try to go to college? Margaret talked to Anna Mae about her situation for a long time, but the two never came to a decision about what she should do.

It was the last time Anna Mae ever saw Margaret. The following Saturday, Margaret, Evelyn, and another cousin named Vela hitched a ride home from a basketball game with a boy who had been drinking. While attempting to pass another car on a hill, the boy collided with a diesel truck heading in the opposite direction. Evelyn and the boy were killed instantly. Margaret was thrown out of the car by the impact and died almost immediately. Only Vela survived the accident.

Anna Mae was at the Hendersons' house when she received word that Margaret and Evelyn were dead. The news was shattering. For a long time after Margaret's death, Anna Mae felt overwhelmed by her loss and by how much she missed her cousin. None of the heartaches and disappointments Anna Mae had endured up until then had as profound an impact as Margaret's death. "That was the first time I realized what hurt was, I think. Real hurt," Tina recalled years later. "I had lost Margaret, and that was like losing a part of my heart."

At Lauderdale High School, Anna Mae had just begun to recover from her grief when she and Alline were sent back to Mama Roxanna's house. Their father had stopped sending support money to Ella

Vera, and she could no longer afford to care for them. Anna Mae enrolled at Carver High in Brownsville, and this time the change did her good. Carver High School principal Roy Bond fondly recalls Anna Mae:

> She was involved in everything. Basketball, cheerleading—she'd be on the court playing, and then she'd go put on a cheerleader's uniform and come back out and lead the cheers for us. If there was a track meet, she'd run track. She would have played football, too, if it had been allowed. She was a leader, an organizer—parties, sock hops, class trips. She might not have been an A student, but she made up for it with her energy.

Anna Mae also participated in school plays, choir, and talent shows. Finally, she began to make new friends and take up typical teenage hobbies, such as listening to music, going to dance mixers, and dating. One boy in particular caught Anna Mae's attention in a big way. His name was Harry Taylor and he became her first true love. Unfortunately, Harry had difficulty being faithful to Anna Mae, and one of the other girls he was seeing became pregnant. When Anna Mae found out from one of her friends that Harry and the girl had gotten married, she cried bitterly.

It seemed to Anna Mae that she could not escape the cycle of feeling abandoned by people she loved. Now, even Alline was moving on, heading to Detroit after her high school graduation so she could live closer to their father. Unwilling to stay with Mama Roxanna in Brownsville anymore, Anna Mae moved back to Mama Georgie's on the Poindexter farm, but her grandmother was not the same woman Anna Mae had adored as a child. Evelyn and Margaret's deaths had made the woman more introspective and withdrawn.

In the summer of 1956, while Anna Mae was on

vacation with the Hendersons in Dallas, Texas, Mama Georgie became ill. She passed away before Anna Mae could return to Tennessee. At the funeral, for the first time in more than five years, Anna Mae saw her mother, who looked even more beautiful than the teenager remembered.

Though she hadn't seen Zelma since her abrupt exit from the family in 1950, Anna Mae had recently begun receiving clothes and money from her. Now, Zelma wanted her daughter to come to live with her in St. Louis. Alline was already there, having left Detroit soon after she arrived.

What was left in Tennessee for Anna Mae? Everyone she loved—Mama Georgie, Harry, Margaret, Alline—had either passed away or moved on. She had missed her mother terribly, though she hated her and loved her at the same time. She finally had the chance to be with the mother she had hoped would someday come back for her. So Anna Mae moved to St. Louis.

4

ST. LOUIS AND
THE KINGS OF RHYTHM

❦

"[Anna Mae's] voice combined the emotional force of the great blues singers with a sheer, wallpaper-peeling power that seemed made-to-order for the age of amplification."

—Clayton Love, former singer
with the Kings of Rhythm

SIXTEEN YEAR-OLD Anna Mae found St. Louis strikingly different from the small towns along Highway 19. The streets were a clamor of automobiles, trolleys, and people coming in and out of shops. To a country girl like Anna Mae, St. Louis was a bundle of lively activity.

Like its sister city across the river, East St. Louis, the city had a thriving night life. Clubs and taverns like the Moonlight Lounge, the Club Imperial, the Blue Note, the Bird Cage, and the Club Manhattan abounded. In the 1950s jazz, blues, and R&B were hot, and artists such as Albert King, Little Milton, and Johnny O'Neal appeared regularly at these venues.

Alline had gotten a job as a barmaid at a high-class club called the Tail of the Cock, where she received generous tips from wealthy patrons. After work, Alline might accompany a date to another top-class nightclub, always traveling in style in Cadillacs and Lincoln Continentals. But on weekends, she and her friends preferred to hang out at more friendly,

Tina and Ike Turner in an early publicity photo. When the 16-year-old girl from Nut Bush first saw Ike, she thought the musician was ugly; when he began to play, however, he seemed transformed. "I was just sitting there, amazed, staring," she later admitted. "I almost went into a trance just watching him."

down-to-earth clubs like D'Lisa and Booker Merritt's Club Manhattan in East St. Louis. Eventually Alline persuaded Anna Mae to join her on their Saturday night outings. Anna Mae was apprehensive at first—after all, she was still a teenager. But she relented, borrowing Alline's clothes and applying makeup so she would look older.

Club Manhattan reminded Anna Mae of one of the bars in the Hole back in Ripley, but it was much larger, with a seating capacity of 200 or 250. A huge crowd—a mixed gathering of white and black fans—had already gathered. As Anna Mae scanned the crowd, a finely dressed black man walked through the room toward the stage. It was the first time she laid eyes on Ike Turner:

> He walked through the room, and everybody was going, "Hey, Ike, hey man," and I thought: "What an immaculate-looking black man." He wasn't my type though—not at all. His teeth seemed wrong, and his hairstyle, too—a process thing with waves that lay right down on his forehead. . . . When he got closer, I thought, "God, he's ugly." But there was something about him. Then he got up onstage and picked up his guitar. He hit one note, and I thought . . . "listen to this guy play." And that joint started rocking. The floor was packed with people dancing and sweating to this great music, and I was just sitting there, amazed, staring at Ike Turner. . . . I almost went into a trance just watching him.

The Kings of Rhythm were one of the hottest bands in the area. Ike was joined by bass player Jessie Knight, vocalist Clayton Love, saxophonists Raymond Hill and Eddie Jones, and drummer Gene Washington. The Kings of Rhythm played countless gigs in and around St. Louis, and by the time Anna Mae first heard them they had already become local celebrities.

The head of the band, Izear Luster Turner, was born on November 15, 1931, in Clarksdale, Mississippi, to Reverend Izear Luster Turner Sr., a Baptist minister, and

Beatrice, a seamstress. The Turners also had a daughter, Lee Ethel, who was 10 years older than her brother. Beatrice Turner taught Ike to sew, a skill the enterprising boy would later use to sell pieced-together fabric samples on the street. He also made money helping a blind man named Mr. Brown navigate Clarksdale. Ike learned to play the guitar from Mr. Brown's wife.

Although Ike had been exposed to the white country music of Nashville, he was drawn to the

Willie "Pinetop" Perkins (second from left, seated at piano) was one of Ike Turner's early inspirations. As a teenager, Ike often sneaked out of the house to watch Pinetop tickle the ivories at a local establishment.

A chance meeting with blues guitarist B. B. King earned Ike Turner and the Kings of Rhythm a meeting with record producer Sam Phillips at Sun Studio. Although the Kings' song "Rocket 88" became a number one hit on the R&B charts, it was credited to a non-existent group called the Delta Cats. Years later, Ike and Tina Turner would join B. B. King as an opening act on a Rolling Stones tour.

blues at a very young age. Many famous bluesmen, such as W. C. Handy, Robert Johnson, Muddy Waters, and Howlin' Wolf made Clarksdale and its neighboring county, Coahoma, home—and Ike lived in the heart of it all. From the intersection of Highways 61 and 49 and the railway station platform in Clarksdale, blues music wound its way north to Beale Street in Memphis, Tennessee, and then up to Chicago, Illinois.

At night, Ike often sneaked out of the house and went downtown to watch boogie-woogie pianist Willie "Pinetop" Perkins jam. Ike watched Perkins and little by little, he taught himself the basics of piano playing. Before long he was able to play from memory one of the riffs he'd seen Perkins perform. While still a teen, he took a job filling in at WROX, Clarksdale's radio station, when the regular deejay took a coffee or soda break.

Soon after, Ike began playing piano for a local swing band called the Tophatters. The pay was meager—sometimes band members made only 13 cents each—but it was valuable experience. When the band broke up around 1948, some of its members joined Ike in forming the Kings of Rhythm.

Ike's band did well locally, but he was eager to expand their reputation beyond the Clarksdale area. In 1951, a chance meeting with Riley B. King (better known as B. B. King) earned them a visit to Memphis to play for King's record producer, Sam Phillips. (A young white kid from Tupelo, Mississippi, named Elvis Presley, would make Phillips famous a few years later.)

With Raymond Hill, Jackie Brenston, Eugene Fox, Willie Kizart, Willie Sims, and Jessie Knight, Ike set up at Phillips's Sun Studio and played a tune written and sung by Brenston called "Rocket 88." Phillips liked the song, and it was released by Chess Records. By June 1951 it had shot to number one on the R&B charts. Unfortunately for Ike, "Rocket 88" was credited to Jackie Brenston and a nonexistent group called the "Delta Cats." Each member of the Kings of Rhythm earned only $20 from the smash hit; Brenston had sold his composer's rights to Phillips for $910. Shortly after recording "Rocket 88," the Kings of Rhythm fell apart. For the next few years, Ike worked as a talent scout for the record label Modern/RPM. It was a lucrative job, but Ike was determined to get the Kings of Rhythm rolling again.

In 1954, Ike accepted an invitation from his sister and her husband to move to St. Louis, Missouri.

After moving to St. Louis, Ike Turner reestablished the Kings of Rhythm, and the band soon developed a local following. This 1964 photo was taken in one of the city's nightclubs, the Bird Cage. On the far left on saxophone is Raymond Hill, the father of Tina's first child, Raymond Craig.

With some of his musician friends in tow, Ike revived the Kings of Rhythm and booked the band at a club in East St. Louis. They were an immediate success. By the time Anna Mae Bullock first visited Club Manhattan, Alline had already met the members of the band, including drummer Gene Washington, whom she was dating. None of them could have imagined that Anna Mae's introduction to Club Manhattan would be the start of a long show-business career.

Anna Mae got to know the members of the band and was soon caught up in the whirl of their wild music and their "celebrity" lifestyle. One of her dreams was to be up on stage singing with the band, and before long she got her chance. During a break in sets one night, Ike played a solo rendition of B. B. King's "You Know I Love You" on the organ. When Gene brought a microphone to the girls' table in an attempt to make Alline sing, Anna Mae took the mike instead. "And boy, Ike—that blew him away," Tina Turner recalled years later. "He went, 'Giiirrrlll!' And he stopped playing the organ and he ran down off that stage and he picked me right up! He said 'I didn't know you could really sing. What else do you know?'" Soon Anna Mae was an occasional vocalist with the band—that is, until her mother found out. Zelma knew of the band's reputation for womanizing and getting into fights, and she forbid her daughter to have any further involvement with Ike Turner and the Kings of Rhythm.

But Ike had big plans, and they included Anna Mae. One day he stopped by the Bullock house to speak directly to Zelma. The band had been booked to perform at a college fraternity party in Columbus, he told her, and Ike wanted Anna Mae to sing. He explained that "away" performances paid good money, far more than the local clubs. Hearing this, Zelma readily gave her permission. Ike promised Zelma that he would take good care of Anna Mae.

The first thing Ike did was buy Anna Mae lots of new clothes—shimmering sequined dresses, long gloves, flashy accessories—to wear when she performed. Suddenly little Anna Mae was traveling around in Cadillacs, wearing sharp, expensive clothes. She felt rich, she felt grand, and she felt important. She viewed Ike as a big brother who took care of his "people." What she didn't realize was that Ike saw his band members and vocalist as elements of a business venture. In his effort to maintain control over his band and its future success, he needed to think for them, make decisions for them, and in a sense, own them.

Anna Mae injected energy and freshness into the band's sound—a development that did not go unnoticed by Ike. The Kings of Rhythm had been a great cover band, but with Anna Mae on vocals the band began to form its own style. Ike knew that national success was within his reach. He had dreamed of performing in venues like the legendary Apollo Theater in New York City, the Howard Theater in Washington, D.C., and the Regal in Chicago, Illinois. For the first time since he recorded "Rocket 88," Ike began to believe this was possible—but to reach that level, the band needed original material.

Ike and Anna Mae's relationship remained platonic. The band leader was a notorious womanizer, and his latest romantic interest was a woman named Lorraine Taylor. Meanwhile, Anna Mae became involved with Ike's pal and band member Raymond Hill, who seemed quieter and more settled than his bandmates. Just after her 18th birthday, while still a senior at Sumner High School, Anna Mae became pregnant. She moved into Ike's home on Virginia Place in East St. Louis, which he called the "house of many thrills," but the arrangement to live there with Raymond didn't last long. Raymond broke his ankle and returned to Clarksdale to recuperate. He never returned.

Anna Mae, still pregnant, moved back into her mother's house. She graduated from Sumner High, and two months later, on August 20, 1958, she gave birth to her first child, Raymond Craig (whom she called Craig). Around this time, Ike also became a parent when Lorraine gave birth to a son, Ike Junior, on October 3.

Not long after her son was born, Anna Mae moved into her own apartment in East St. Louis. She continued to sing with the band every night, earning $15 per week. She also took a job as a nursing assistant, caring for newborns at Barnes Hospital. Handling two jobs in addition to taking care of her own infant son was extremely difficult for the teenage mother. With no real career skills, Anna Mae became dependent on Ike not only for financial support but also for advice on the music business. "Ike made me feel important and I don't think there was anything I might have wanted at that time that Ike wouldn't have given me," she recalled in her autobiography. "And that kind of confidence was a foundation for me, for the first time in my life—a kind of family love."

Ike's strictness and desire for control frequently put him at odds with his band, and members came and went frequently. Eventually, Anna Mae moved back into Ike's house with her son. Although she did not realize it at the time, her decision would mark the beginning of 17 years of professional success and personal torment.

5

A FOOL IN LOVE

⚫⚫

"I think she has tremendous ability not to just sing the song, but to act the song, that really injects her personality into it. . . . There [are] great singers around, but she's also a great actor of the song."

—Terry Britten, co-author of "What's Love Got To Do with It"

ANNA MAE'S VOICE first appeared on a recording with Ike and the Kings of Rhythm in 1958, in a tune called "Box Top" that was released on a St. Louis label. Although the record had little impact on the music charts, in live performances Anna Mae's unique vocals attracted a great deal of attention. She was especially popular among white youngsters, who in the late 1950s were becoming captivated by the pulsating beat and raw energy of black R&B music.

Bonnie Bramlett was among these teenagers. She even briefly became an Ikette, the name Ike Turner gave to his backup singers. In *I, Tina*, Bramlett recalled how she felt when she first heard the Kings of Rhythm and Anna Mae's voice:

I thought she was the greatest thing I'd ever seen in my life. She made me cry—yeah: I stood there and cried like an idiot. I knew right away that that was what I wanted to do, too. And I wanted to do it just like her. . . . Ike Turner used to be madness then,

Publicity shots portraying Tina and Ike as a happy couple belied the physical and emotional pain Tina was suffering at the hands of her husband.

swinging his guitar, kicking his leg up. . . . Then came the Revue—all the singers, and everybody doin' steps—and they created a whole lot of excitement. . . . The whole place would just pulsate. I mean, the Kings of Rhythm were a big, humpin' band, you know?

Ike and Anna Mae continued to interact with one another as friends. At times, she would accompany him to clubs, where they would meet other people in the business, observe other bands, and set up new gigs. Ike seemed to have no personal interests that didn't concern his work, and this gave Anna Mae the chance to learn the ins and outs of the music business.

But then, during a breakup with Lorraine, Ike seduced Anna Mae. The two felt very awkward about the change in their relationship, but Anna Mae, seeking to erase her feelings of abandonment, fell in love with Ike. A 20-year-old single parent, Anna Mae had few other options than to stick with Ike and perform with the Kings of Rhythm. And besides, she knew beyond a doubt that she wanted to sing for a living. Ike had the band and the know-how to give her that opportunity.

But Ike returned to Lorraine and fathered another child with her, a son named Michael, in February 1959. And even though Lorraine moved back into the house on Virginia Place, Ike wanted Anna Mae to continue to be his mistress. Anna Mae found that arrangement unbearable, even more so when she discovered that she too was pregnant with Ike's child.

Depressed and confused, she moved out of Virginia Place and rented a small house in another part of town. Anna Mae began struggling with a new emotion: she had come to feel that she owed Ike her loyalty. Ike deeply resented people like Jackie Brenston, whom he faulted for deserting him and not giving him credit. Anna Mae vowed she would never do that to Ike, yet a

long-term relationship with him—a house, kids, and a life like the Hendersons'—just didn't seem possible.

Unaware of Anna Mae's struggles, Ike remained consumed by his music, landing gigs for the band and tapping out new tunes on the piano when they weren't performing. His quest for the hit song that would catapult the Kings of Rhythm into stardom finally produced one—although under circumstances that neither Anna Mae nor Ike could have imagined. Ike had been working on a song called "A Fool in Love" that had a lead male vocalist part for Art Lassiter, a singer with the Kings of Rhythm. Ike recalled years later:

Anna Mae Bullock's vocals finally gained national attention for Ike Turner when she recorded "A Fool in Love" with the Kings of Rhythm. Ike had wanted to use a male vocalist, but record producer Henry Murray insisted that Anna Mae was the group's star attraction.

I had booked the recording studio . . . [but] he didn't show up at the session, and [Tina] . . . she knew the song. . . . The studio was about $25.00 an hour in those days. . . . After he didn't show . . . I said [to Tina] well, "you sing it." . . . So I asked the guy, "Well man can you put the band on one side [of the two-track recording] and put her on the other one so when I find this guy we can erase Tina's voice and put him on it?" And he said yeah. . . . I played the tape out at the Club Imperial in St. Louis where I was workin' at, and all the kids said "Man that's great, put it out, put it out, put it out," and so Dave Dixon a disc jockey . . . said that he was gonna give it to Juggy Murray at Sue Records and he did man and so, boom, the damn thing was a hit.

Henry "Juggy" Murray was one of the few blacks in the music business who owned and operated his own record label. In its first year, the label had a hit

Ike Turner felt that his lead singer's name was not interesting enough; remembering a film he had seen as a child called Sheena: Queen of the Jungle, *featuring an exotic heroine (left), he told Anna Mae that she would be called "Tina" professionally. For the Revue's performances, he also dressed her in skimpy outfits that the film character might have worn (right).*

song, "Itchy, Twitchy Feeling" by Bobby Hendricks. Though many of his contemporaries considered Juggy Murray egotistical and slightly eccentric, he also had an ear for music and knew a hit when he heard it. Murray flew to St. Louis to meet with Ike and signed him up for a $25,000 advance. Ike still wanted to rerecord "A Fool in Love" with a male lead vocalist, but Murray told him to forget it; it was Anna Mae's voice that made the song. He suggested that Ike take a closer look at his fill-in singer. Murray firmly believed that Anna Mae was the star attraction of the Kings of Rhythm.

After Ike closed the deal with Murray, he told Anna Mae that "A Fool in Love" would be released with her vocals, but not under her name or the Kings of Rhythm. Instead, it would be credited to Ike and Tina Turner. Who was Tina Turner? Anna Mae wondered. Ike explained that her own given name was not exciting enough now that they were about to hit the big time. She needed a more catchy name. Remembering the name of one of the primitive beauties in a "jungle" film he saw as a child—*Sheena, Queen of the Jungle*—he came up with Tina. That was it, he told Anna Mae. Wild and provocative Tina Turner. Anna Mae was less than pleased. "I wasn't into changing my name," she recalls. "We used only Tina for the work, and then everyone still called me Ann."

With the name change came a terrifying new phase in Anna Mae's relationship with Ike. It was shortly after the release of "A Fool in Love" that she first became the target of Ike's uncontrolled rage. To prepare for the success of his new hit song, Ike decided to move to Los Angeles, California. Tina was reluctant to go. When she tried to explain her misgivings to Ike, he became enraged and began beating her with a shoe stretcher. Bruised and bloodied, with one eye swollen, Tina listened in shock as Ike told her how it was going to be between them. *They* were going to California, he said. He would pay her expenses, but he would keep the rest of the money for himself.

Stunned and frightened, Tina acquiesced. Perhaps in time, she thought, she could make things better between them. Maybe if she loved him enough he would stop his womanizing. If she could help him grab the brass ring of success, he would be happy. She was too afraid to consider the alternatives.

"A Fool in Love" climbed the pop charts quickly

in the summer of 1960 and received a great deal of air time. But the excitement was lost on Tina who, while still pregnant, contracted hepatitis severe enough to land her in the hospital for six weeks. Lying in her hospital bed listening to the radio, Tina heard the song over and over again, like an echo of herself:

> Boy, I got to hate that . . . song. I'd have to lie there, all sick and swollen up [pregnant], and listen to "A Fool in Love" every day, and I'd be thinking—it sounds funny now, but it's the truth—I'd be thinking: "What's love got to do with it?" You know? Because here I was, pregnant by Ike Turner, who's gone back to his wife, and now she's getting suspicious. . . . I mean, this was not my idea of love at all.

Impatient to get on the road and capitalize on the success of the hit single, Ike told Tina that she had to leave the hospital, despite what the doctors advised. He sent one of the band members to pick her up, and she sneaked out of the hospital in the middle of the night. The Ike and Tina Turner show was on the road by the following morning, headed for Cincinnati, Ohio, where they were opening for Jackie Wilson.

By August 1960, "A Fool in Love" had peaked at number two on the R&B charts, and the newly named Ike and Tina Turner Revue was landing gigs in bigger and more prestigious clubs and theaters, including Harlem's Apollo Theater. That fall, Ike and Tina were invited to perform on Dick Clark's nationally televised teen dance show, *American Bandstand*. They had made it to the top at last.

But the big time was not always glamorous. In addition to well-known venues, the Revue also played in smaller, less accommodating clubs. Often back stockrooms became makeshift dressing rooms, where Tina and the Ikettes had to put their makeup on in near darkness and sit on beer cases while getting dressed.

While preparing for one such performance in a

Ike, Tina, and the band spent much of their time on the road performing wherever they could, including small, cramped clubs and dance halls such as this one. It was not unusual for the band to travel 700 miles between one night's performance and the next. With Tina's powerful voice and stage energy, the Revue's first hit, "A Fool in Love" (1960), was quickly followed by another, "It's Gonna Work Out Fine."

run-down locale in Las Vegas, Ike finally noticed that Tina was in the last stage of her pregnancy. Worried that she would go into labor while they were on the road, Ike canceled the date and took her back to Los Angeles. The next morning, October 27, 1960, Tina delivered her second child, Ronald Renelle Turner. It didn't take long for Lorraine to realize that Ronald was Ike's child. Fed up with his promiscuousness, Lorraine walked out for good, leaving their sons, Ike Jr. and Michael, for Ike to care for.

Tina herself was embarrassed by her pregnancy and upset that she was partly the cause of Lorraine's anger and disgust. She was exhausted from the grueling work hours Ike demanded of her. When they weren't performing, they were on the road headed to the next show or in a studio recording. They rehearsed constantly, it seemed—on the bus, in hotel rooms, in the car—whenever they weren't sleeping, eating, or performing.

Tired, paranoid, and irritable from lack of sleep, Ike had little patience with Tina. Grabbing anything within arm's reach—a shoe, a belt, a coat hanger—he repeatedly struck her when she didn't sing a song exactly the way he wanted her to. Tina carried constant reminders of his brutality—black eyes, a busted lip, lumps on her head. With every move, she feared she would set him off again. When the Revue's second pop hit, "It's Gonna Work Out Fine," faded from the music charts, Ike's beatings increased.

It was becoming clear that the raw energy of Tina's voice and her electrifying stage presence had kept the Ike and Tina Turner Revue from being just another run-of-the-mill party band. Ever the shrewd businessman, Ike intensified his control over Tina; he knew he could not afford to have her leave the band. He asked Tina to marry him. In fear of another beating, Tina agreed. She had really wanted to say no, to scream it from the depths of her soul, but she couldn't.

With Ike and the bus driver, Duke, she traveled to Tijuana, Mexico, to find a justice of the peace. Tina had expected a beautiful, lush country, but the narrow dirt roads they drove along did not offer such a view. Finally, they saw a "marriage" sign in front of a dusty, dingy building in a small town. A man slid a piece of paper across the table for Ike and Tina to sign and pronounced them married.

This was her wedding. Tina, Ike, and the bus driver as a witness. No honeymoon, no romance, no anything. What should have been the happiest day of Tina Turner's life was instead just another in a string of countless days filled with disappointment, unhappiness, and growing despair.

6

RIVER DEEP,
MOUNTAIN HIGH

— ❦ —

"She could just do anything. She was like working with a perfect instrument."

—record producer Phil Spector

THE MOVE TO Los Angeles became permanent after Ike purchased a large ranch house in a predominantly white section of the city known as View Park Hills. Now that Ike and Tina had a large home, they brought all four of the boys—Ike Jr., Michael, Craig, and Ronnie—and a housekeeper to live with them.

The Ike and Tina Turner Revue toured virtually year-round, and it was not unusual for the band to log 700 miles in a 24-hour period between gigs. All together, nine months of each year were dedicated to this grueling schedule. Unwilling to spend money on road crews or a business manager, Ike took control of every aspect of the tours. He required band members to set up and break down their own instruments and load their own equipment on and off the bus.

Before long, however, the work became too much even for Ike and his crew to handle, so he hired Ann Cain, whom he had discovered working in a local record shop on La Brea Avenue. Ann not only "clocked the gate" (watched club owners take money at the door to be sure they weren't cheating Ike out of his earnings) but also assumed the responsibility of caring for the boys when the housekeeper quit. She

In 1966, top-notch producer Phil Specter invited Tina to work with him on her first solo recording. The result, "River Deep, Mountain High," was a smash hit in England, and it made Tina realize that she could be successful without Ike Turner.

55

managed to transform the spoiled, unruly children into relatively well-mannered, disciplined young men. Impressed by her skills in organizing his family, Ike began taking Ann on the road.

Ann was one of the few people who witnessed the extent of Ike's continual mistreatment of Tina. Ike had become savage, often burning his wife with lit cigarettes or throwing hot coffee in her face. During one fierce argument, he fractured her ribs. It became part of Tina's routine to wear sunglasses and use make-up to hide her injuries for photo sessions and performances. For her, the one saving grace was that the beatings usually occurred while the band was touring, so the children were not exposed to the violence.

In 1987, an interviewer for *Ladies' Home Journal* asked Tina Turner why she stayed with Ike despite his brutality. "I was afraid of him," she replied. "I didn't fight back, because I thought it would be over quicker if I didn't. . . . It was very painful to try to sing half the time with a fractured nose and a busted lip and a black eye, but I just sang. I can't explain it. You wonder how soldiers keep fighting when they're wounded," she continued. "That's what it was like. You don't know why, you just hope maybe it will get better, and you go on. And then the busted lip is gone."

Tina no longer had the strength or the courage to fight Ike's philandering. Though the constant parade of women in and out of Ike's life hurt Tina emotionally, her main concern was to keep her husband's physical assaults to a minimum by trying not to upset him. Once Ike started using drugs, however, his already volatile temper became even more deadly.

The Ikettes introduced Ike to illegal drugs, particularly marijuana. Although Tina tried marijuana once, she did not like the sensation and has stayed drug-free ever since. But it was just the beginning of Ike's fascination with drugs. His substance abuse made him more violent and irrational than ever, and he terrorized not only Tina but also everyone else around him.

The Turners and their children: Tina and Raymond Hill's son Craig (top right), Lorraine and Ike Turner's sons, Ike Jr. (top left) and Michael (bottom left), and Ike and Tina's son, Ronnie (bottom right).

Although the Ike and Tina Turner Revue was still in great demand as a touring band, it had not managed to repeat the recording successes of "A Fool in Love" and "It's Gonna Work Out Fine." In desperation, Ike switched from one record label to another in search of his next hit single. Around the same time, a 24-year-old named Phil Spector was changing teen rock and roll with a new method of studio recording known as the "wall of sound," using multiple guitars, basses, and pianos in a single recording session to create an imposing and majestic sound.

Spector had already worked with such well-known groups as the Righteous Brothers, the Crystals, and the Ronettes, and by the end of 1965 he was looking for a new voice. The first time he heard Tina singing with the Revue, he knew he had found it. He invited the Revue to participate in a taped program called the *Big TNT Show,* filmed at the Moulin Rouge club in Los Angeles. Other performers included such big-name stars as the Byrds, Ray Charles, and Petula Clark. The Revue brought down the house.

Phil Spector collaborated with the New York pop-recording team of Jeff Barry and Ellie Greenwich to create a song called "River Deep, Mountain High." Then he called Bob Krasnow, head of Ike's most recent label, and told him that he wanted to work with Tina alone. Spector insisted that Ike not accompany Tina to any of the studio recording sessions.

Tina was thrilled by the opportunity to work solo. Someone had finally taken note of *her* talents, and for the first time in her career she was being treated like a professional. She also greatly enjoyed the relaxed atmosphere of the studio, a refreshing change from Ike's constant harangues and beatings.

"River Deep, Mountain High" was so different from anything Tina had ever performed that she immediately fell in love with the song. And Phil wanted her to sing in her normal voice, not screaming and shouting, as Ike insisted she do when performing with the Revue. "It was my voice he liked, not the screaming," Tina recalled in her autobiography. "He told me I had an extremely unusual voice, that he had never heard a woman's voice like mine, and that that was why he wanted to record me." The project was a great psychological boost for Tina. Working with Phil Spector provided an oasis from the harsh, grind-it-out life of touring and living with Ike.

Hearing "River Deep, Mountain High" for the first time was a bittersweet moment for Ike. He was excited by the technology involved in making the song—this was what he had always wanted to do himself—but the fact that Phil Spector had completed the process of recording and producing without input from Ike was a blow to his ego.

By late spring of 1966 the song was finally ready for release. Early previews by others in the business were positive. But the record ultimately reached no higher than 88 on the American pop charts before disappearing altogether. This failure took everyone by surprise, especially Phil Spector, who was convinced that "River Deep, Mountain High" was his best work so far. Most accounts blame the song's failure on music business "politics," but Tina herself claims that the song "never really found a home" among pop or black audiences because it was too much of a mix of musical styles.

Nevertheless, Tina was buoyed by the experience. She had proved that she was capable of a much greater musical range than the stable of songs to which Ike had restricted her. And the song did become a smash hit in England, reaching number three on the charts and remaining in the top 50 for 13 weeks. The Rolling Stones, who had followed the American group long before "River Deep, Mountain High" became a hit, invited the Revue to travel with them as an opening act.

This was the first time either Ike or Tina would perform outside of the United States, and the experience was electrifying. The gritty, soulful sounds of blues and

Legendary Rolling Stones' front man Mick Jagger met Tina Turner when the Revue was hired as the Stones' opening act in 1966. After more than 30 years, the two maintain a close friendship.

R&B music were becoming ragingly popular in England. Ike and Tina had never before encountered such audience enthusiasm. Mick Jagger, the lead singer for the band, explains how their opening act challenged and inspired his own band to aim even higher: "They would really work the audience very, very hard. But that's the reason we had them on. There's no point in having some jerk band on before you—you have to have somebody that'll make you top what they do. And Ike and Tina Tuner certainly did that job admirably."

Tina Turner the performer was doing very well. Anna Mae Bullock, however, was lost. She didn't have time to spend socializing and attending parties with members of the Revue and the Rolling Stones. She didn't even know who Mick Jagger was. Tina had never seen the Stones on stage; she spent most of her free time sewing, repairing, or ironing her costumes for the next performance, and her emotional energy was directed toward fending off beatings from Ike and keeping herself together for performances.

Eventually, however, Tina did meet Jagger, and he soon began visiting her and the Ikettes in their backstage dressing room. Mick loved hanging out with "the girls" from America. What he really wanted was to learn how to do Tina's trademark strut, known as "the pony," and incorporate the energy of her onstage presence into his own performances. This casual friendship would turn out to be one of the most important relationships in Tina's professional and personal life.

On a whim one afternoon when Tina had a few free hours, she visited a psychic who read people's fortunes in tarot cards. "I'll never forget what she told me," Tina said of the card reader. "She said, 'You will be among the biggest of stars . . . and your partner will fall away like a leaf from a tree.'" The woman also told her that the number six had significance. "I held onto what that reader said," Tina remembered, "knowing my time would come, knowing that someday I'd be free of this life I was leading."

When the tour with the Rolling Stones was finished, Ike and Tina traveled to France and Germany to make press and television appearances. Tina was especially drawn to the culture and language of France, and for the first time she began to feel as though she were "home." The trip to England had been the "beginning of everything" for Tina Turner— it offered an escape from Ike and an ember of hope for a life of her own.

7

YOU SHOULDA
TREATED ME RIGHT

❦

"[Tina] like a Phoenix from the ashes has risen. . . . She's
certainly been through far worse than many of us have been
through, and has been able to survive it. And it's that element
of resoluteness and discipline, and just not letting the world
take over, that people respect. . . . I think she's got an
enormous amount of dignity."

—David Bowie, who sang "Tonight,"
a duet with Tina Turner

THE SUCCESS OF "River Deep, Mountain
High" brought Tina greater recognition not only in
England but also in the United States. And because
this meant more money, Ike was undisturbed by
Tina's rise in celebrity status. At the same time, he
had gotten so brazen about his philandering that
Tina actually found him with another woman in
their home.

Tina was now looking for a way out of her marriage, but she wasn't sure how she could manage it.
She had tried to escape Ike once a few years earlier
by sneaking away on a bus headed to St. Louis. But
Ike tracked her down before the bus arrived there,
forced her to get off, and later beat her for trying to
leave him. She knew how hard it would be to try
getting away from him again.

The situation worsened when all the band members, fed up with Ike's abuses, simply quit, leaving

*After 17 years of abuse, Tina
Turner finally felt strong
enough to break away from Ike
Turner and strike out on her
own. "I always like to say that
I graduated from the Ike Turner
Academy," she said in her
autobiography, "and that I took
care of all my homework before
I left him."*

Ike to find a whole new crew to keep the Revue going. One of the new musicians was a baritone sax player named Johnny Williams. Williams was a well-mannered and well-dressed man, and he behaved like a real gentleman. Tina was instantly attracted to him. For once, she felt she had something to look forward to, someone whose company she enjoyed and with whom she could talk and hang out while on the road.

But unfortunately Tina and Johnny's friendship ended soon after it began. After Tina received a particularly vicious beating from Ike, Johnny saw the condition she was in and started to cry, right up on stage. Without saying a word, he put his saxophone down and walked off. The next day, Ike received Johnny's resignation letter, in which he said that he could not work for a man as brutal as Ike.

With Johnny gone, Tina slid even further into despair. When she became pregnant again, she terminated her pregnancy. She hit bottom in 1968. Shortly before a concert performance, the 28-year-old tried to commit suicide. She had convinced her doctor that she needed medication to help her sleep, and he had prescribed Valium. Before she left home that day, Tina swallowed the entire bottle of 50 pills. She took one last look around the house and left for the Apartment, a new black club in Los Angeles.

Tina planned to begin her performance and collapse on stage, so that Ike would still get paid for the gig. But the Ikettes noticed that Tina was acting strangely in the dressing room before the show. Someone called Rhonda Graam, the road manager, to come backstage. Graam vividly remembers what she saw:

> Tina was there putting eyeliner on, and running it all the way down her cheekbone. I said, "Duh-Duh [Tina's nickname], what did you do?" I couldn't really get an

answer from her—it was like, "I took shum shleepin' pillzhhh," you know? . . . Then Ike came in, and he got mad. He tried to get her to throw up; then he said, "Get the car, we're taking her to the hospital."

There the emergency team pumped Tina's stomach, but it was some time before she was out of danger. Her first sight upon awaking was Ike, who immediately began cursing her and accusing her of trying to ruin his life. In disbelief that her plan had failed and she remained trapped with Ike, Tina simply turned away.

The Rolling Stones's 1969 concert tour, for which Ike and Tina Turner opened, was dubbed "the best rock show ever presented." "Tina Turner must be the most sensational female performer on stage," the noted music critic Ralph Gleason commented. But though Tina remained professional and upbeat onstage, her personal life was filled with abuse, loneliness, and despair.

Only a few days later, Ike forced Tina to return to performing. Still feeling weak, Tina fought waves of nausea. It hurt to sing; her stomach muscles and her throat were sore. But Ike showed Tina no sympathy. For the first time since she had met him, Tina began to loathe the man who called himself her husband.

By 1969 the Ike and Tina Turner Revue was landing ever classier gigs and opening for such megastars as Elvis Presley. Though her personal life was still a shambles, Tina had forged friendships with several celebrities, including actress and singer Ann-Margret, who was a big fan of Tina's.

In search of a hit song, Ike renewed his relationship with record producer Bob Krasnow. The Revue's cover of Otis Redding's "I've Been Loving You Too Long" became the first significant hit for Ike and Tina in several years. But it was R&B, and Tina was growing bored with the style. She had begun listening carefully to the latest pop hits—singles such as the Rolling Stones's "Honky-Tonk Women" and the Beatles's "Come Together," both of which had reached number one on the charts during the late summer and fall of 1969. Tina loved the new "rock and roll" sound. R&B, she thought, was depressing, but rock and roll was fun, it was full of energy, and it was naughty. Somehow Tina persuaded Ike to add a cover of both of these songs to their repertoire. For Tina, this marked the beginning of a new phase in her career:

> It wasn't like we planned it—"Now we're gonna start doing white rock and roll songs." But those groups were interpreting black music to begin with. They touched on R&B, in a way, but it wasn't obvious. I mean, it wasn't the old thing. It was "Honky-Tonk Women"—wow! I could relate to that.

In November, the Ike and Tina Turner Revue joined B. B. King on the Rolling Stones's 13-city

American tour. It was the first chance for the Revue to try out their new sound on a large-scale live audience. The tour, which kicked off in Los Angeles, was a huge success. Ralph Gleason, a respected pop and jazz critic and cofounder of a new music magazine called *Rolling Stone*, praised the concert as being perhaps the "best rock show ever presented." The critic reserved his highest accolades for the Ike and Tina Turner Revue—especially for Tina herself:

> After B. B. King's set came World War III. Or rather Ike and Tina Turner. In the context of today's show business, Tina Turner must be the most sensational

Bored with the standard R&B fare of the Revue, Tina convinced Ike to incorporate rock and roll covers from groups like the Beatles (above) and the Rolling Stones into their act.

female performer on stage. . . . She comes on like a hurricane. . . . She dances and twists and shakes and sings and the impact is instant and total. . . . She did blues, of course, but the number that really wiped out the house was her version of "Come Together," the John Lennon song from the Abbey Road album. It was a most surprising and effective performance.

Clearly, Tina Turner was beginning to develop a rock and roll style, and more important, her *own* style, that was separate from that of Ike and his Revue.

In 1970, Ike signed with Minit Records, with whom he would work for the remainder of the Revue's career. That year the band had a remarkable four songs in the Top 100: "Bold Soul Sister" at 59th in January, their versions of "Come Together" and "Honky-Tonk Women" each at 57th in April, and in August, "I Want To Take You Higher" at 34th. The money came pouring in, and Ike was deliriously happy.

Tina, however, became very ill. Unwilling to cancel a single gig, Ike pushed her to continue to perform. Finally, she felt so feverish one night that she drove herself to the hospital, where she was initially diagnosed with pneumonia and a collapsed lung. After she also developed painful lumps in her legs, Tina was diagnosed with tuberculosis. Several years would pass before she fully recovered.

The following January, with Tina back on the road but still weak, the Revue reached their all-time high when their cover of the Creedence Clearwater Revival song "Proud Mary" was released. By March, it had soared to number four on the charts, becoming their biggest hit ever, and by May it had sold over a million copies. The song would ultimately earn Tina her first Grammy Award (as half of the Ike and Tina Turner Revue), but the significance of the song went even deeper for her. In *Tina Turner: The Girl from Nut Bush*, Tina explained what having a hit rock and roll song meant: "Escape. My first time that I actually ad-libbed on stage, the beginning part of it. It's my song. It was always my song," she declared.

"Proud Mary" earned more money than Ike had ever seen, and he used much of it to fulfill his life-long dream of owning his own recording studio, which he dubbed Bolic Sound. But a great deal of the earnings from the song was also spent on Ike's substance abuse. His cocaine use increased, and he would often stay up for days after a coke binge, working on music tracks in the studio. It was not unusual for Ike to summon Tina to the studio at three in the morning for a recording session.

But the drug also made Ike even more volatile and violent. If Tina didn't sing a note exactly as Ike thought it should sound, he would go on a tirade, hitting her and throwing things at her. Tina held on by remembering what the card reader had told her years before: "You will be among the biggest of stars . . . and your partner will fall away like a leaf from a tree."

There would be only one more hit for the Ike and Tina Turner Revue, an upbeat dance number called "Nut Bush City Limits," based on Tina's childhood home. By November 1973, the song reached number 22 on the American pop charts, and in England it held at an astonishing number two for almost three weeks. Unnoticed by most fans and reviewers was the song credit: Anna Mae Bullock, the private persona of the public per-former, Tina Turner. As the band earned more fame, Tina had become more involved in the nuts and bolts of the business, and she believed that having a song of hers reach the top of the charts would assuage Ike and help him feel successful. Only then, she believed, would she be able to earn her freedom from him.

One day Ike introduced Tina to a woman named Valerie Bishop, the wife of a black jazz musician he knew. Though Jewish in heritage, Valerie practiced Buddhism, and Ike, who was fascinated with witchcraft and black magic, believed that her chanting was just another kind of occult practice. Neither Ike nor Tina could have imagined, however, that the introduction to Valerie would bring Tina back to life and give her the strength and conviction to escape Ike for good.

Looking back, Tina believes that Valerie Bishop was sent to Tina expressly to teach her a form of religion known as Nichiren Shoshu Buddhism, which is based on the teachings (or Lotus Sutra) of a 13th-century Japanese priest named Nichiren. Members of this sect strive to understand that the individual and the environment are interconnected and inseparable, and thus each human being has an impact on both. Every thought, word, or action affects the person and his or her environment, even if the effect takes time to become apparent. The goal of Nichiren Shoshu Buddhism, Valerie told Tina, is to achieve a level of enlightenment that allows one to understand this interconnection. Only then can a person reach his or her full potential as a human being and channel the energy to others.

Valerie gave Tina a book describing Buddhism and a set of the beads she used while chanting. She also taught her the chant phrase: "nam-myo-ho-renge-kyo." Eager for emotional and spiritual solace, Tina took to the practice immediately. She procured a *butsudan* (a small cabinet) to house the *Gohonzon* (scroll of the law of Nam-myoho-renge-kyo), and she read and chanted before the Gohonzon daily, feeling herself grow stronger, more self-assured, and confident.

Tina Turner believes that the positive turn of events that occurred after she began chanting was a direct result of her new spiritualism. In 1974 the

The success of the rousing "Proud Mary," which became Ike and Tina Turner's biggest hit when it reached number four on the Billboard chart in 1971, enabled Ike to fulfill his long-time dream of establishing his own recording studio.

Revue was without a hit, but Tina herself was approached by record producer Robert Stigwood, who invited her to play the part of the "Acid Queen" in the film version of *Tommy*, a 1969 rock opera by the British group the Who. Tina joined a cast that included stars such as Oliver Reed, Jack Nicholson, and her Las Vegas pal, Ann-Margret. And once again, as with Tina's recording of "River Deep, Mountain High," Ike was not asked to participate.

Tina was thrilled not only to sing on film but also to try her hand at acting. "I loved doing

Tina as the frightening Acid Queen in the 1975 film version of the rock-opera Tommy. *"I loved doing* Tommy," *she later said in her 1986 autobiography. "It gave me strength."*

Tommy," she said in her autobiography. "My part was small, but it was *my* part. It gave me strength. I could feel myself growing."

Perhaps in fear of Tina's increasing independence, Ike took out his aggressions on nearly everyone in sight. It seemed to Tina that he was angry with the entire world. One night after what Ike believed was an unsuccessful recording session, he threw scalding coffee at Tina. She sustained third-degree burns on her neck and face. He had become "anger itself," she recalled years after.

By mid-June of that year, Tina began to view herself as an individual, a performer in her own right. More and more, she imagined herself "Ike-less." Looking back over her life, she could see that she had evolved in "stages of seven":

> From birth to age seven, childhood. From seven to fourteen, school years, girlhood. Fourteen to twenty-one, first love—ah, Harry Taylor—and then meeting Ike, becoming a singer. From twenty-one to twenty-eight, falling in love with Ike, then becoming his prisoner and feeling that love begin to ebb. In the years from twenty-eight to thirty-five, [I] had finally come to hate the man. Now on the verge of thirty-six, [I] felt that a massive transition was at hand, an end to all old things and a beginning of the new.

Confident of her own worth, Tina began planning her final escape from Ike.

As it happened, Tina Turner achieved her independence on the very day that America itself was celebrating 200 years of freedom—July 4, 1976. That day the Revue was scheduled to be in Dallas to kick off yet another regional tour. Having gone without sleep for several days after a cocaine binge, Ike was in a particularly paranoid and combative mood. But Tina was no longer inclined to step lightly around Ike. Sixteen years of pent-up anger was about to burst open.

8

SIMPLY THE BEST

❦

"I think Tina Turner is a legend, a personification of a survivor and an endurer. Tina Turner—unforgettable."

—Singer Al Green, whose song
"Let's Stay Together" became one
of Tina Turner's biggest hits

One of the most successful comebacks in rock and roll history: Tina Turner electrifies her audience during a 1995 solo performance.

IN THE LIGHT of day, Tina realized that although she had escaped Ike for the moment, she was far from being truly free of him. With a canceled show and a missing lead vocalist, Ike would not only be seething with rage but would also be looking for her. She knew that Ike would contact everyone he could think of, including her sister, Alline, and her mother, Zelma, to track her down, so she decided to call Nate Tabor, Ike's attorney, for help. From Los Angeles, Tabor made arrangements to have her driven to the Dallas airport, where an airline ticket to L.A. would be waiting for her.

Tina stayed with the Tabors for a week. At the end of the week, Tabor called Ike to tell him that Tina wanted a divorce. Incensed that Tabor would dare harbor Tina, Ike threatened to harm him and his family. Tina was unwilling to put her hosts in jeopardy, so she moved to the home of her friend Maria Booker, who lived in Southern California. For the next few months, Tina continued to shuttle from

Turner in one of the lavish costumes she wore while performing on the cabaret circuit. These show performances, without the backing of her former husband and band, helped her to get back on her feet financially and provided a stepping-stone to her career as "Queen of Rock and Roll."

Inferno" and tunes from the hit movie *Saturday Night Fever*. After a long and difficult struggle to be on her own, she was now getting regular work. But the cabaret circuit was tough and didn't pay much. Now almost 40 years old, Tina knew she didn't want to do cabaret forever.

Her big break came with an invitation from singer Olivia Newton-John to appear on her television special, which had been launched after Newton-John's successful appearance in the smash hit movie *Grease!* After the TV special, Tina approached Lee Kramer, Newton-John's manager, to see whether he would represent her. Kramer took Tina to meet his partner, Roger Davies.

It didn't take much to convince Davies to take her on. "Her dream was to fill stadiums," he said, and he believed that she had the talent to do it. One of the first things he did was to change her "look." This included getting rid of her long hair, her glittery costumes, and even her backup band and sound technicians. What Tina Turner needed, Davies believed, was a more youthful band whose members had grown up on rock and roll and who were hungry to create their own sound.

In the United States, Tina Turner was a relative unknown, remembered only for the now-dated music she had performed with the Ike and Tina Turner Revue. Davies knew that Tina needed exposure before a new generation of rock fans. In the summer of 1981, Davies convinced Jerry Brandt, the owner of the Ritz, one of the hottest clubs in New York City, to book Tina. Brandt's only outlay was the cost of hotel rooms and payment for Tina's band members.

Brandt widely advertised Tina's appearance, and he invited an array of stars to Tina's show—including Mick Jagger, artist Andy Warhol, singer Diana Ross, and actors Robert DeNiro and Mary Tyler Moore. The August show was such a smashing success that Davies was able to line up a return appearance in

October. Among the celebrities who attended Tina's second concert was Rod Stewart, who was scheduled to host the late-night TV program *Saturday Night Live* that weekend. Stewart was so impressed with Tina that he invited her to appear on the show with him. In front of an audience of millions of TV viewers, Tina and Stewart performed a duet of his hit song "Hot Legs." Finally, Tina Turner was in the right place at the right time—and before the right audience. In the brief time it took to sing Stewart's song, she had gotten the exposure she and Davies had been hoping for.

Later that fall, Turner and Davies traveled to Los Angeles to see the Rolling Stones, who were in the midst of a U.S. tour. The Stones congratulated Tina on the *Saturday Night Live* appearance and invited her to open for them on the remaining nights of their tour. This was the moment Tina Turner had been waiting for: she performed for a crowd of 20,000 people each night, and some of the biggest names in the music industry attended. When Mick Jagger invited Tina to join him in a rendition of the Stones hit "Honky-Tonk Women," they brought down the house.

In just a few years away from Ike Turner, Tina had made a name for herself as a musical "legend." Her next goal was to land a recording contract. Once more, her British connections in the music business would be the key to achieving a full-fledged comeback. Martyn Ware and Ian Craig Marsh, two computer operators from Sheffield, England, had formed a production company called British Electric Foundation (BEF), dedicated to developing electronically synthesized music. While working on a multi-artist album called *Music of Quality and Distinction*, they contacted Davies about having Tina record a cover of the Temptations's "Ball of Confusion."

Well-prepared as always, Tina walked into BEF studios and blew Ware and Marsh away. Though the

Tina and Roger Davies attend a birthday party for Mick Jagger's wife in 1986. Davies, who has been Tina's manager since 1979, is largely credited with engineering Tina's spectacular comeback. "We have a lot of trust between each other," Davies says. "There's been a lot of energy and a lot of trust. . . . I've loved every moment of it."

album was never released in the United States, it created quite a buzz in England—so much so that Davies approached Capitol Records (the American company owned by EMI in England) to discuss a recording contract for Tina. Unfortunately, just before the deal was closed in mid-1983, Capitol underwent a serious management shakeup, and the agreement was delayed indefinitely.

Davies didn't let up, however. He increased Tina's public exposure to critics, music executives, and rock fans. In her return engagements at the Ritz, Tina continued to draw huge crowds, and it was there that she finally received the break she and Davies were looking for. The boost came from another British rocker, David Bowie, who had recently signed a recording contract with EMI/Capitol Records. Bowie was in town for a listening party to launch his new album, *Let's Dance*, and he told Capitol Record executives that he was going to a performance of his "favorite female singer, Tina Turner." Eager to please Bowie, Capitol called Davies and requested that he add 63 names to the guest list for that evening's show. That night, Bowie, the executives from EMI/Capitol International, and an assortment of celebrities including Susan Sarandon, Keith Richards, and tennis great John McEnroe attended the concert. Tina, as usual, was fantastic.

EMI/Capitol wanted Tina to record a single immediately. Davies booked recording time at Abbey Road studios in London with Martyn Ware and Ian Craig Marsh, where in just one take Tina recorded a cover of Al Green's 1971 hit "Let's Stay Together." By December 1983 the single reached number five on the British charts.

Although the domestic branch of EMI/Capitol had been decidedly lukewarm about Tina's marketing potential, they changed their tune when "Let's Stay Together" started receiving air time in the United States. By February 1984 the song was in the Top 40 on the American charts, and Capitol wanted an entire album from Tina. Davies was stunned. He had already booked her for more than 30 performances in Europe, leaving little time to produce an album. But Capitol insisted.

With only a few weeks to assemble an album, Davies quickly called in favors from business acquaintances and Tina's British connections. While Tina toured, he collected songs. In an on-line interview with *MusicCentral*, Davies described the frantic process:

Rocker David Bowie dances with Tina during the filming of a 1987 commercial for Pepsi-Cola. Four years earlier, Bowie's interest in the woman he called "my favorite female singer" led Capitol Records to offer her a recording contract. The result was her smash hit album Private Dancer.

We finished this month of dates and then . . . recorded the *Private Dancer* album in three weeks, from start to finish, using several producers: Rupert Hine, Terry Britten, the Crusaders, Martyn Ware. . . . We'd be in one studio during the day with one producer, then at night we'd go to another studio with another producer. At the end, I had no idea if the album would jell, I didn't know if it would have any thread [of continuity].

Tina played Mel Gibson's nemesis in the apocalyptic film Mad Max: Beyond Thunderdome, *the highly anticipated 1985 sequel to the surprise Australian hit* The Road Warrior *(1981).*

The songs that made the final cut included "Better Be Good to Me," "Let's Stay Together," "Steel Claw," "What's Love Got To Do with It," "I Might Have Been Queen," and the album title song, "Private Dancer." Davies need not have worried about whether the album sounded unified. Though *Private Dancer* is a mix of pop, reggae, electro-funk, and hard rock, and though it was cut in several locations with a number of producers, Tina's powerful and soulful voice was the strong thread that tied it all together. By the time the album was released in mid-June 1984, the single "What's Love Got To Do with It" was already rapidly climbing the pop charts.

In 24 years of performing, Tina Turner had never had a number-one hit record. That was about to change. In August, "What's Love Got To Do with It" moved to the top of the charts, prompting Tina to scream "My record's number one! My record's number one!" when she received the good news during a promotional appearance at New York City's Tower Records. The fans who had gathered in the store to see her broke into loud cheers and applause.

Suddenly Tina Turner was hot news. Just the day before, Davies had gotten a call from Australian film director George Miller, who had heard about Tina and wanted her to appear in his next Mad Max film, *Beyond Thunderdome*. Eager for the chance to prove her versatility, Tina gladly accepted the part of a woman warrior named Entity.

The rest of that year was a whirlwind of activity. Tina made numerous talk-show appearances and a number of radio and telephone interviews. Music videos of her newest songs played regularly on MTV. In September, *Private Dancer* reached number three on the pop charts, in good company behind two other megahit albums, Prince's *Purple Rain* and Bruce Springsteen's *Born in the U.S.A.* At the same time, two other songs from her album were Top 10 singles. All told, *Private Dancer* went platinum, selling more than 10 million copies, and yielded five American Top 10 singles—including, of course, her first number-one hit.

After completing some performance obligations, Tina flew to Australia to begin filming with costar Mel Gibson in *Mad Max: Beyond Thunderdome*. But though Tina greatly enjoyed the experience and loved acting, she later turned down Steven Spielberg's invitation to star in the film version of Alice Walker's novel *The Color Purple*. Referring to the protagonist's lifelong struggle to overcome physical abuse at the hands of her stepfather and husband, Tina remarked, "I've *lived* that story." (The part was given to Whoopi Goldberg instead.)

If 1984 proved that Tina could make a musical comeback, 1985 showed that she was in the business to stay. In January she won Best Female Vocalist and Best Video Performer awards at the American Music Awards ceremony. Immediately following the program, she joined 46 singers, songwriters, and actors, including Michael Jackson, Lionel Richie, Diana Ross, Billy Joel, and Dan Ackroyd in an unprecedented recording session at A&M Records to raise funds to fight hunger in Africa and the United States. The single, "We Are the World," was a spectacular success, earning nearly $50 million in proceeds.

That year, Tina Turner was also nominated in five categories by NARAS. In what was heralded by *Variety* magazine as "one of the most dramatic comebacks in music history," Tina reached the high point of her solo career, walking off with three Grammys, including Best Female Pop Vocal Performance and the coveted Record of the Year award for "What's Love Got To Do with It." On July 13, 1985, Tina joined Mick Jagger on stage in Philadelphia, Pennsylvania, to participate in a colossal two-continent concert benefit known as Live Aid.

In the years just after her breakthrough into rock, Tina continued to tour. In 1986 she released a second solo album, *Break Every Rule*. Shortly after that, she launched a massive 18-month world tour, beginning in Europe and traveling to the United States and South America. At one of her appearances, a concert at Maracana Stadium in Rio de Janeiro, Brazil, Tina Turner played to the largest paying audience in history, a crowd of more than 182,000 people. The concert was broadcast live via satellite by HBO, and an album of her concert appearances, *Tina Live in Europe*, was released in 1988.

Now Tina had realized yet another dream—to fill stadiums—and she hadn't arrived there by being a sidekick for someone else or having good looks. "When you have drawn that kind of a crowd," Tina said of the

Tina with her longtime companion, Erwin Bach. "The relationship is a very healthy one,"
Tina said in 1989. "It's not restricting . . . and we still live our own lives."

Rio de Janeiro concert in the documentary video *Tina Turner: The Girl from Nut Bush*, "you're not embarrassed that somebody's putting a stamp on you cause you can say 'Okay, then what is superstardom?' . . . If I'd never filled that [stadium], I don't think I would feel it from just [having] big hair, lips, and legs. You have to have some credibility there, and now I have that credibility."

Tina released another album, *Foreign Affair*, in 1989. Two years later, *Simply the Best*, a collection of her greatest hits, was released. That same year she and Ike Turner were both inducted into the Rock and Roll Hall of Fame. Now 52, Tina decided she deserved a break and took two years off from touring and performing.

Around this time Disney Studios approached Tina for the rights to film her life story, which she had described in the 1986 book *I, Tina*, written with Rolling Stones journalist Kurt Loder. The motion picture, entitled *What's Love Got To Do with It*, starred Angela Bassett as Tina and featured Laurence Fishburne as Ike Turner. Ike himself, who was serving an 18-month jail term for cocaine possession, expressed bitterness at having been portrayed in the film as a "bad guy," claiming that the root of his and Tina's marriage problems stemmed from his drug use.

At first, Tina was hesitant about having the private events of her life portrayed on screen. Before long, however, she became excited by the project. Her only frustration came from the repeated question, "Why did you stay with Ike for so long?" The question missed the point, she thought. "I was in control every minute there. I was there because I wanted to be, because I had promised," she said in a 1993 interview with *Vanity Fair*. "O.K. . . . maybe I was a victim for a short while. But give me credit for *thinking* the whole time I was there," she insisted. "See, I do have my pride."

"What's reality sometimes is not exactly real," Tina continued. "Because you keep saying, 'What did I do?' You get on your knees every night and you say the Lord's Prayer, and you say 'Somebody must send some help to me, because I've never done a thing in my life to deserve this.'"

After touring to promote the film and its music, Tina took another break from performing, during which she moved to Germany with her longtime companion, Erwin Bach, an executive with EMI Records. Though he was almost 20 years her junior,

A sure sign of success: Tina performs on the long-running late-night TV program Saturday Night Live *in February 1997.*

Turner shows off the watercolor that she created for Novus's Private Issue credit cards in 1997. The painting depicts Tina's life journey from Nut Bush, Tennessee, to her home in Southern France.

Tina felt an instant connection with Erwin. "The chemistry just happened and we have been together ever since," Tina said in a 1989 interview. "And the relationship is a very healthy one. It's not restricting; it's not demanding, and we still live our own lives." At the same time, Tina purchased two other homes, one in Zurich, Switzerland, and another in the south of France—the country where, years earlier, she declared that she felt right at home from the time she arrived.

She was prompted to emerge from her retreat when the producers of the newest James Bond epic, *GoldenEye*, asked her to record the title track for the film. In 1996, at age 57, Tina released a new album, *Wildest Dreams*, and launched her tour of the same name, the most ambitious of her solo career. The album—a blend of rock, pop, and R&B—was written and produced by U2, the Pet Shop Boys, and Sheryl Crow, and features duets with Antonio Banderas and Sting. In search of a "fresh, yet classic" sound, Tina hired British record producer Trevor Horn to update her arrangements. Why the name *Wildest Dreams*? "Because, fortunately," Tina replied, "all of mine have come true."

Having been voted the female celebrity with the sexiest legs, it seemed only natural that Tina's grand tour would be sponsored by Hanes Hosiery. In the first product endorsement of Tina's 40-year career, national TV and print campaigns spotlighted not only her physical features, but also her personal strength. "I'm resilient. I'm confident. I feel beautiful," Tina declared in the ads.

In May 1997 Tina exhibited a different side when she unveiled an original watercolor painting entitled *Southern Connection* as part of a Novus credit card "Private Issue" celebrity series. The painting depicts Tina's life as a winding journey from Highway 19 in Nut Bush to her present home in France. At the unveiling ceremony, Tina said, "For many years I have been recognized for my voice, my dancing and yes, for my legs. It's refreshing to be appreciated for my artwork. To have my art appear on a credit card that thousands of people can own and enjoy is exciting. It's an opportunity for me to share the pleasure I derive from art with others."

The *Wildest Dreams* tour was yet another triumph for the veteran performer. Kicking off the tour in Paris on May 3, 1996, Tina performed 250 shows in 45 cities around the world without a single cancellation. The tour ended in July 1997 with a spectacular concert at the famed Radio City Music Hall in New York City.

These days, the woman dubbed the Queen of Rock and Roll divides her time shuttling between her homes in Zurich, Switzerland, where she enjoys the city's comfortable size and variety of shops, and the south of France, where she spends relaxing hours decorating and puttering in her garden. Still a practicing follower of Nichiren Shoshu Buddhism, Tina finds great comfort in the faith that helped her through her darkest years.

Tina Turner's reputation as rock and roll's sexiest, most energetic female vocalist stems from her sheer love of performing. Even through the long years of exhaustive, one-night gigs and physical abuse, she remained the ultimate professional whose every performance was electrifying. Along the way she has collected three generations of fans and six solo Grammy Awards—and she has never looked back. In a December 1998 interview with SwissTV, Tina said that she plans to release another album in the near future. She'd also like to tour again, but she would prefer to appear in more intimate settings than the huge arenas and stadiums she has filled in the past.

So now that her wildest dreams have come true, what's in store for Tina Turner? In an interview with Grant Giles of *QX* magazine, the "true queen of survival" answered the question with characteristic simplicity. "The next part of my life is just keeping that [success] in perspective," she says. "To retire on top of the world would be beautiful."

Along the road to stardom: a triumphant Tina Turner poses on her Harley Davidson in 1993.

CHRONOLOGY

1939	Anna Mae Bullock born November 26 in Nut Bush, Tennessee, to Floyd Richard and Zelma Bullock
1941	The Japanese attack Pearl Harbor, Hawaii; the United States enters World War II
1942	Floyd Richard and Zelma Bullock move to Oak Ridge, Tennessee; Anna Mae is sent to her paternal grandparents, Roxanna and Alex Bullock
1950	Zelma Bullock leaves her husband and moves to St. Louis, Missouri, leaving Anna Mae and sister, Alline, with Floyd Richard
1953	Floyd Richard moves to Detroit, Michigan, leaving behind his daughters
1954	Cousin Margaret is killed in a car accident
1956	Maternal grandmother, Georgianna, dies; Anna Mae moves to St. Louis to live with Zelma and Alline Bullock; meets Ike Turner at a St. Louis nightclub
1958	Gives birth to Raymond Craig on August 20; the father, Raymond Hill, a saxophone player in Ike's band, leaves shortly after; cuts her first recording, "Box Top," with Ike and the Kings of Rhythm
1960	"A Fool in Love" reaches number two on R&B charts; Ike changes Anna Mae's name to Tina and renames the band the Ike and Tina Turner Revue; Tina gives birth to Ronald Renelle on October 27
1962	Marries Ike Turner
1966	With Phil Spector as producer, releases her first solo single, "River Deep, Mountain High"; the Revue tours abroad as the opening act for the Rolling Stones
1968	Attempts suicide
1970	The Revue has four Top 100 hits; Tina is diagnosed with tuberculosis
1971	"Proud Mary" hits number four on the music charts, earning Ike and Tina a Grammy Award
1974	Appears as the Acid Queen in the film version of *Tommy*
1976	Leaves Ike; they divorce in 1978

1979 Signs up Roger Davies as manager

1984 First solo album, *Private Dancer*, released; "What's Love Got To Do with It" becomes her first number one hit; appears in *Mad Max: Beyond Thunderdome*; wins two American Music Awards

1985 Wins three Grammy Awards: Best Female Pop Vocal Performance and Record of the Year for "What's Love Got To Do with It," and Best Female Rock Vocal Performance for "Better Be Good to Me"; wins MTV Music Video Award for Best Female Video, "What's Love Got To Do with It"

1986 Meets German record company executive Erwin Bach; second solo album, *Break Every Rule*, is released; wins Grammy, Best Female Rock Vocal Performance for "Back Where You Started"; shares MTV Music Video Award for Best Stage Performance with Bryan Adams for their duet, "It's Only Love"; publishes autobiography, *I, Tina: The Tina Turner Story*; is named to Hollywood Walk of Fame on August 28

1989 Wins Grammy Award, Best Female Rock Vocal Performance for *Tina Live in Europe*; third album, *Foreign Affair*, is released

1991 With Ike Turner, inducted into the Rock and Roll Hall of Fame; *Simply the Best* is released

1993 Disney releases film *What's Love Got To Do with It*, based on Tina's autobiography

1996 Awarded the Chevalier of Arts and Letters medal, France's most prestigious cultural honor

1996–97 *Wildest Dreams* is released; embarks on *Wildest Dreams* tour, playing 250 shows in 18 months

1998 *Live in Amsterdam: Wildest Dreams Tour* video nominated for Best Music Video, Long Form

Tina Turner beams as she receives a star on the Hollywood Walk of Fame in August 1986.

DISCOGRAPHY

ALBUMS

Private Dancer (1984)

Break Every Rule (1986)

Tina Live in Europe (1988)

Foreign Affair (1989)

Simply the Best (1991)

Collected Recordings: Sixties to Nineties (1994)

Wildest Dreams (1996)

DUET SINGLES

"Tonight" (with David Bowie)

"It's Only Love" (with Bryan Adams)

"Tearing Us Apart" (with Eric Clapton)

"634-5789" (with Robert Cray)

"It Takes Two" (with Rod Stewart)

"In Your Wildest Dreams" (with Barry White)

SOUNDTRACK SINGLES

"Acid Queen" (*Tommy*)

"Johnny & Mary" (*Summer Lovers*)

"Crazy in the Night" (*Summer Lovers*)

"We Don't Need Another Hero" (*Mad Max: Beyond Thunderdome*)

"One of the Living" (*Mad Max: Beyond Thunderdome*)

"Break Through the Barrier" (*Days of Thunder*)

What's Love Got To Do with It (complete album)

"GoldenEye" (*GoldenEye*)

BIBLIOGRAPHY

Cossette, Pierre. *The 27th Annual Grammy Awards*. Produced by Ken Ehrlich. Directed by Walter C. Miller. 180 min. Cossette Productions, Inc., 1985. Videocassette of awards telecast on CBS television.

Davies, Roger. *Tina Turner: The Girl from Nut Bush*. Produced & directed by Chris Cowey. 100 min. EMI Records Ltd., 1992. Videocassette.

du Lac, J. Freedom. "Ike Turner Putting Tina Behind Him." *Sacramento Bee*, 19 September 1997.

Gundersen, Edna. "Wildest Dreams Do Come True." *USA Today*, 15 May 1997.

Harrington, Richard. "What's Age Got To Do with It?" *Washington Post*, 21 June 1997.

Hilburn, Robert. "Tina's Comeback Tops Grammys." *Los Angeles Times*, 27 February 1985.

Hirshey, G. "Tina Turner." *Rolling Stone*, 13 November 1997.

King, Larry. "Interview with Tina Turner." *Cable News Network*, 21 February 1997.

McGuigan, Cathleen. "The Second Coming of Tina." *Newsweek*, 10 September 1984.

Mower, Sarah. "Private Tina." *Harper's Bazaar*, December 1996.

Norment, Lynn. "Tina Turner." *Ebony*, September 1996.

Orth, Maureen. "The Lady Has Legs!" *Vanity Fair*, May 1993.

Pareles, Jon. "Tina Turner, 58 and Still Kicking." *The New York Times*, 25 July 1997.

Pennypacker, Ramsey. "Rollin' on the (Delaware) River." *Philadelphia Weekly*, 9 July 1997.

Rubenstein, Hal. "Tina Turner: Her Least Nostalgic Interview, Ever." *Interview*, August 1993.

Sporkin, Elizabeth. "Tina Turner: Her Most Candid Interview." *Ladies Home Journal*, April 1987.

Tina Turner Live in Amsterdam: Wildest Dreams Tour. Produced by Monique Ten Berge & Patrick Roubroeks for IDTV. Directed by David Mallet. 122 min. Eagle Rock Entertainment, 1997. Videocassette.

"Tina Turner." Rock on the Net. Internet (http://www.rockonthenet.com/artists-t/tinaturner_main.htm), 23 February 1998.

Turner, Tina, with Kurt Loder. *I, Tina: My Life Story*. New York: Avon Books, 1986.

Wynn, Ron. *Tina: The Tina Turner Story*. New York: Macmillan Publishing Company, 1985.

INDEX

PICTURE CREDITS

page

2: Reuters/Corbis-Bettmann
3: AP/Wide World Photos
10: AP/Wide World Photos
13: © Ann Summa/London Features International
16: © Sharon Norris/Nutbush Heritage Productions
18: © Sharon Norris/Nutbush Heritage Productions
19: © Harrell E. Clement
22: UPI/Corbis-Bettmann
24: UPI/Corbis-Bettmann
27: © Sharon Norris/Nutbush Heritage Productions
29: © Sharon Norris/Nutbush Heritage Productions
30: © Sharon Norris/Nutbush Heritage Productions
34: Michael Ochs Archives/ Venice, CA

37: courtesy Stephen C. LaVere/Delta Haze Corporation
38: UPI/Corbis-Bettmann
40: courtesy Stephen C. LaVere/ Delta Haze Corporation
44: Michael Ochs Archives/ Venice, CA
47: Michael Ochs Archives/ Venice, CA
48: Photofest
49: Michael Ochs Archives/ Venice, CA
52: Michael Ochs Archives/ Venice, CA
54: Michael Ochs Archives/ Venice, CA
57: Michael Ochs Archives/ Venice, CA

60: Corbis-Bettmann
62: Michael Ochs Archives/ Venice, CA
65: Michael Ochs Archives/ Venice, CA
67: AP/Wide World Photos
71: Photofest
72: Photofest
76: AP/Wide World Photos
80: © London Features International
83: Corbis-Reuters
85: AP/Wide World Photos
86: Photofest
89: © David Fisher/London Features International
91: Photofest
92: Photofest
95: Corbis-Reuters
98: AP/Wide World Photos

The author wishes to extend special thanks to Erin Riley for her help in obtaining "the tape," and to Rob Hyman for digging through boxes to find and share it. My deepest gratitude to you both for assisting me with this project.

JUDY L. HASDAY, a native of Philadelphia, Pennsylvania, received her B.A. in communications and her Ed.M. in instructional technologies from Temple University. A multimedia professional, she has had her photographs published in many magazines and books, including a number of Chelsea House titles. As a successful freelance author, Ms. Hasday has written several books for young adults, including an award-winning biography of James Earl Jones, and a biography of Madeleine Albright. She also co-authored *Marijuana* in Chelsea House's Junior Drug Awareness series.

NATHAN IRVIN HUGGINS, one of America's leading scholars in the field of black studies, helped select the titles for the BLACK AMERICANS OF ACHIEVEMENT series, for which he also served as senior consulting editor. He was the W. E. B. DuBois Professor of History and Afro-American Studies at Harvard University and the director of the W. E. B. DuBois Institute for Afro-American Research at Harvard. He received his doctorate from Harvard in 1962 and returned there as professor in 1980 after teaching at Columbia University, the University of Massachusetts, Lake Forest College, and the California State University, Long Beach. He was the author of four books and dozens of articles, including *Black Odyssey: The Afro-American Ordeal in Slavery*, *The Harlem Renaissance*, and *Slave and Citizen: The Life of Frederick Douglass*, and was associated with the Children's Television Workshop, National Public Radio, the Boston Athenaeum, the Museum of Afro-American History, the Howard Thurman Educational Trust, and Upward Bound. Professor Huggins died in 1989, at the age of 62, in Cambridge, Massachusetts.

HARBORFIELDS PUBLIC LIBRARY

3 0632 00057 3463

DISCARDED

jB
TURNER

Hasday, Judy L.,
1957-

Tina Turner.

$19.95   MAR   2000

DATE			

HARBORFIELDS PUBLIC LIBRARY
31 BROADWAY
GREENLAWN, NEW YORK 11740

BAKER & TAYLOR